The Socio-Economic
Approach to Management
Steering Organizations into the Future

The Socio-Economic Approach to Management

Steering Organizations into the Future

John Conbere
Alla Heorhiadi
SEAM Institute, USA

NEW JERSEY · LONDON · SINGAPORE · BEIJING · SHANGHAI · HONG KONG · TAIPEI · CHENNAI · TOKYO

Published by

World Scientific Publishing Co. Pte. Ltd.

5 Toh Tuck Link, Singapore 596224

USA office: 27 Warren Street, Suite 401-402, Hackensack, NJ 07601

UK office: 57 Shelton Street, Covent Garden, London WC2H 9HE

Library of Congress Cataloging-in-Publication Data

Names: Conbere, John P., author. | Heorhiadi, Alla, author.

Title: The socio-economic approach to management : steering organizations
into the future / by John Conbere (SEAM Institute, USA), Alla Heorhiadi
(SEAM Institute, USA).

Description: New Jersey : World Scientific, [2018] | Includes bibliographical references and index.

Identifiers: LCCN 2017051597 | ISBN 9789813232983 (hc : alk. paper)

Subjects: LCSH: Management--Social aspects. | Employee motivation. |
Organizational change.

Classification: LCC HD30.19 .C66 2018 | DDC 658--dc23

LC record available at https://lccn.loc.gov/2017051597

British Library Cataloguing-in-Publication Data

A catalogue record for this book is available from the British Library.

For any available supplementary material, please visit
http://www.worldscientific.com/worldscibooks/10.1142/10788#t=suppl

Desk Editors: Chandrima Maitra/Yulin Jiang

Typeset by Stallion Press
Email: enquiries@stallionpress.com

Printed in Singapore

Foreword

Just 20 years ago, we, the founders and proponents of the socio-economic approach to management, decided to go to the United States, which is often considered in France as "the management temple," in order to spread our research results. The Academy of Management allowed us to meet colleagues, teachers and researchers who have become our friends and colleagues. They discovered in our works a stimulating opportunity for interactions because SEAM challenges the dominant management models in the United States and all over the world. This French–US cooperation resulted in several English publications, which the readers can find at the end of this book.

With the kind participation of our colleague and friend David Boje, Professor at the University of New Mexico, we first published a special number of the periodical *Journal of Organizational Change of Management* in 2003. David Boje and Grace Ann Rosile also urged us to spread our works in the United States, in particular, works on SEAM and intervention-research method.

Anthony F. Buono, Professor at Bentley University and the Director of the Research in Management Consulting collection at the Information Age Publishing, discovered ISEOR's works during a sabbatical leave in Lyon (France). He suggested that we publish some of our major results, drawing on what is now more than 1,800 cases of SEAM application in companies and organizations in 42 countries around the world and in

72 business sectors over 43 years. This cooperation led to two original books co-published by Anthony Buono and Henri Savall on SEAM: the first in 2007 (*The Intervener-Researcher and the SEAM Approach to Organizational Analysis*) and the second in 2015 (*The Socio-Economic Approach to Management Revisited: The Evolving Nature of SEAM in the 21st Century*). Simultaneously, Anthony Buono and George Johnson, IAP editions managers, supported us in translating into English our French and Spanish books which had been published since 1975 in order to increase the dissemination of SEAM in the Anglo-Saxon world and, in particular, in the United States. The list of the major works, published for last 15 years, also appears in the bibliography in this book.

In addition, an original book was written by Véronique Zardet, Marc Bonnet and Amandine Savall with our colleague Christopher Worley, researcher at the University of South California (*Becoming Agile — How the SEAM Approach to Management Builds Adaptability*). It was published in 2015, drawing on the case study of Brioche Pasquier, a French company that became international and has applied SEAM for more than 30 years.

Two other books are in progress: with our colleague Robert Gephart, Professor at the University of Alberta (Canada), to show how SEAM constitutes a crisis prevention and management method, and with Murray Lindsay, Professor at the University of Lethbridge (Canada), to show how SEAM questions the traditional management control methods.

Our colleagues Peter Sorensen and Thérèse Yaeger, Professors at the University of Benedictine (Chicago), have been active partners in scientific conferences that we organize in Lyon, France, in partnership with the Management Consulting and Organizational Change and Development divisions of the Academy of Management. We collaborated with them to compare change management approaches.

John Conbere and Alla Heorhiadi's book is the 12th SEAM book published in English. It is part of a collective work of spreading the SEAM method and management theory in the United States that began 20 years ago. The originality of their book is based on the fact that it is written by two North American colleagues from their understanding and own experience of SEAM. The book presents the principles and the fundamental tools of SEAM in a language and concept that is adaptable to the North

American mindset. It is about the adaptation of SEAM in the United States, with a double vision from their background as academics and practitioners. Indeed, our colleagues John Conbere and Alla Heorhiadi are the first ones who led complete intervention-researches using the SEAM model in North American companies and organizations. Thereby, their book presents, in particular in Chapters 6 and 7, applications of SEAM in different American organizations: healthcare, universities, transport services, non-profit organizations. The last two chapters of the book are particularly illuminating and bring a major added value for readers who wish to understand SEAM. Why does SEAM remain a management method which is not in the mainstream? What are the conditions needed so that SEAM can be applied in North American companies?

This book is addressed to students, teachers and researchers, management, change management or organizational development consultants, managers and directors of companies. You will discover that SEAM is a "think tank" in management. It contains a strong criticism of the classic scientific management approaches. It highlights the mistakes due to the traditional accounting model and suggests the concept of hidden performance and cost, as well as the operational method. These hidden costs which result from organizational dysfunctions are, certainly, intuitively perceived by the shareholders, the directors, managers, employees and customers. But as these costs are never calculated, their importance is widely underestimated. It leads companies to erroneous decision-making which, finally, explains why companies do rarely succeed in getting their expected economic performance. For example, profitability analyses which prepare merger and acquisition decisions, never integrate human, social and organizational dysfunctions, which are going to occur after the (legal) merger and are going to reduce the expected profitability.

To those who may think that SEAM is a method suited for companies and organizations which do badly, consider that SEAM is a relevant method for ANY company or organization. Indeed, whatever the financial results are, every organization suffers from hidden costs situated between $20,000 and $70,000 per person per year. These hidden costs represent a reserve which can be tapped to improve the economic performance. SEAM gives organizations the chance to convert somewhere between 35% and 55% of these hidden costs into added value. SEAM also enables organizations to improve their performance without implementing strategies that are based only on cost-cutting. SEAM leads to economic performance improvement for short, medium and long terms by activating the only lever of human potential development of companies and organizations. This approach can be applied in companies of any size (from 2 to 30,000 persons), any legal status (public, private or non-profit), or any country.

SEAM represents, thus, a managerial philosophy, including principles on the development of human potential and on strategic and organizational creativity and innovation. SEAM is a long-term strategic development method for the company, in which the roles and implications of all actors from the manager to the most modest employee are modified.

As explained by John Conbere and Alla Heorhiadi, this book will not be enough for you to apply SEAM. We hope that it stimulates your curiosity and enables you to discover SEAM, a management approach that was designed by us and applied continuously for 43 years.

Henri Savall
Professor Emeritus, the founding President of ISEOR,
Laureate of Moral and Politic Sciences Academy (French Institute),
the Legion of Honor award in the rank of Chevalier
from the Ministry of Education, Higher Education, and Research

Véronique Zardet
Professor at iaelyon, Jean Moulin University,
France, Director of ISEOR
Laureate of Moral and Politic Sciences
Academy (French Institute)

A Word from a SEAM Client

Being a CEO, I wonder:

Why wouldn't a leader want to tap into human potential?

Why wouldn't a leader want to reduce dysfunctions?

Why wouldn't a leader create an environment that respects and values all team members?

Why wouldn't a leader create an organization that can thrive?

Why wouldn't a leader want to lead or invest in sustainable change?

I believe that no matter how well an organization is run, there is always an opportunity to become even better. I realized this by learning about SEAM and challenging self to be vulnerable and open to an organizational transformation. What I have learned through the SEAM journey is that there is no shortage of dysfunction. Dysfunctions are everywhere. This also means there are opportunities to improve everywhere.

When we started our SEAM journey, the first intervention was in the C-Suite. It was through the intervention process (interviews — Mirror Effect — hidden costs — Expert Opinion — baskets — selecting projects) that the C-Suite addressed dysfunctions and root causes of the problems. Though it was difficult at the time, we gained knowledge and skills that made us better team players. The learning through reflection with coaching support made us all better leaders. I wish I would have experienced this socio-economic approach decades ago, before all the bad habits developed. Many of those bad habits were caused by the TFW Virus.

After the leadership team went through a change, we continued to cascade SEAM down through multiple functional silos of the organization. I was present at every feedback session in each silo, which gave me a wealth of information I did not know before. I have also witnessed a general consistency in baskets that tried to address the same root causes of many different problems. I saw how employees wanted to be engaged in improvement projects because they knew it would improve their everyday work. Instead of feeling hopeless, they became active in reducing dysfunctions in their own departments and across other departments in the organization. As a result, involvement in the change process gave employees an opportunity to develop. Since there was a lot of untapped potential in employees, the change in the process allowed to uncover this potential in a different form and manner. This released potential triggered change throughout the organization.

SEAM is a long-term commitment. There is no quick fix. Those who believe that sustainable and radical changes may happen in a few months, may be delusional. It will take 3–5 years for change to cascade throughout an organization to ensure it becomes part of the cultural fabric. I witnessed the outcome of SEAM in my organization — culture change. This culture change was not imposed; it happened not because someone proclaimed it. It was an iterative process — people began to believe they are heard and respected. And because they felt heard and respected, they took ownership of change, they took on new initiatives, and modeled change for those who still did not go through SEAM intervention. I can say that SEAM healed the workplace and created a more vibrant organization.

I am glad that SEAM is translated and adapted to American mentality. I am thankful that I was introduced to SEAM — it opened my eyes to a new way of work and management. I wish more leaders were exposed to SEAM, for their own sake as well as their organizations.

Dave Dobosenski
CEO,
St. Croix Regional Medical Center, Wisconsin

Preface

The socio-economic approach to management, or SEAM, was developed in 1973 in Lyon, France, by Henri Savall. He created the socio-economic theory as part of his doctoral thesis and since then, he kept fine-tuning this theory. SEAM has become a separate discipline, taught at the Université Jean Moulin Lyon 3 in Lyon. In 1975, Savall created a research institute named ISEOR where he teamed up with likeminded colleagues to develop the discipline and train students, so they could lead SEAM interventions in organizations. ISEOR stands for *Institut de socio-économie des entreprises et des organizations* (the Socio-Economic Institute of Firms and Organizations). Savall has authored as well as co-authored many books and articles, and in 2016, he was awarded the French Legion of Honor for his work by the Ministry of Education, Higher Education, and Research in France.

We were teaching organization development (OD) and doing OD consulting in organizations when, in 2006, we were introduced to SEAM. Since then, we have become converts of SEAM. We have attended numerous ISEOR seminars and conferences, designed and taught classes on SEAM, and carried out SEAM interventions in different organizations in three states. In order to share and spread knowledge about SEAM, we have formed a professional association of SEAM, organized annual SEAM conferences in the US for academics and practitioners, and launched an online journal about socio-economic theory and practice.

One of the reasons we shifted from the field of OD to SEAM is that in our opinion SEAM could overcome the limitations of other disciplines such as OD, change management, and management consulting. First of all, SEAM is a very effective and sustainable organizational change methodology. Second, this methodology is based on a research database of the organizational changes accumulated by ISEOR over more than 40 years. Every intervention is a research case and ISEOR keeps records on all interventions led by the ISEOR members or its franchises. At the time of writing this book, there have been over 1,800 interventions in 72 industries, across the 42 countries, and only two of the interventions failed. Such high success rate confirms the SEAM theory, which Savall crystallized in the mid-1970s and has kept expanding. Most importantly, SEAM is based on the belief that organizations must attend to both the human and economic aspects of work, which make an organization both ethical and efficient.

We wrote this book because while SEAM appears very simple, its simplicity is deceptive. There are many components that are happening at the same time, and there are theoretical premises for each action. It may take some time to put everything together to understand the whole, specifically, the philosophy, change methodology, and change tactics. In France, ISEOR prepares intervener-researchers by apprenticing them. Students and junior intervener-researcher first watch and then participate in the process, delivered by experienced intervener-researchers, and finally lead interventions under the watchful eye of the ISEOR faculty. This is an effective way to bring new people into the field, but it only works if one lives close to Lyon and speaks French. For those who live far away or do not speak French, this training method does not work.

Our intention was to help those English speakers, who want to learn about SEAM, yet cannot travel to France to study the discipline. We need to warn that this book alone will not prepare someone to do full SEAM interventions. However, the reader will get an understanding of socio-economic theory and may be able to apply some elements of SEAM in the workplace or in practice. We should add that there are some healthy organizations, wonderful workplaces, and excellent managers. They probably do not need a SEAM intervention, although they might benefit from learning about the SEAM philosophy and practice.

Organization of the Book

This book was not easy to write. The socio-economic approach to management, or SEAM, is complex and multidimensional, as it includes three domains — socio-economic theory, SEAM change intervention, and SEAM management. To make the book easy to follow, we have metaphorically taken a three-dimensional (3D) geometrical shape and unfolded it flat into two-dimensional (2D) surface areas. Each face of the 3D "SEAM shape" is discussed through a different lens in different chapters, to facilitate the readers' understanding. After reading about every facet of SEAM, the reader's task will be to put all concepts together and to recreate a holistic picture of SEAM.

Thus, this is how this book is organized. Chapter 1 provides a quick summary, a bird's eye view of the points of differentiation that make SEAM unique and distinctive from other management and consulting approaches.

Chapter 2 elaborates on the core concepts of SEAM. Understanding these concepts allows the reader to see the reasoning behind every step of the SEAM intervention process.

Chapter 3 describes the theory and steps of a SEAM intervention.

Chapter 4 describes the SEAM management tools. To help the reader understand the tools better, each tool is discussed in the following manner: the purpose of the tool, a description of how to use the tools, explanation of what makes the SEAM tools different, the link of the tool to socio-economic theory, and some examples to illustrate the use of the tool in organizations.

Chapter 5 discusses the theoretical roots that influenced the socio-economic theory.

Chapter 6 is based on the observations from implementing SEAM in the US. It explores two major organizational problems and shows how SEAM can address these problems.

Chapter 7 provides some insights into organizational culture and transformative learning. The chapter argues that SEAM fosters a new culture through transformation of all actors.

Chapter 8 suggests several reasons why SEAM is not well known in the US.

Chapter 9 describes the ethics and spirituality of SEAM.

About the Authors

John Conbere, MDiv, EdD, is President of SEAM, Inc., which is the only company in the US licensed by ISEOR to conduct SEAM interventions. He was a Professor of Organization Development at the University of St. Thomas in Minneapolis, MN, where for many years he was Department Chair and Director of the doctoral program. Conbere has international teaching and consulting experience, mostly in France and Ukraine. With Alla Heorhiadi, he has co-authored a number of articles on SEAM and organizational change, many of which can be found at www.seaminstitute. org. He is Co-director of the SEAM Institute, and co-editor of two books on SEAM. Before working in OD, Conbere was an episcopal priest, mediator and conflict management consultant.

Alla Heorhiadi, PhD, EdD, is Vice President of SEAM, Inc., Co-director of the SEAM Institute, and Chief Editor of the online, peer-reviewed journal, *The Theory & Practice of Socio-Economic Management*, which is available at www.seaminstitute.org. Heorhiadi is a scholar-practitioner and has versatile teaching and consulting experience in the US and abroad. She has taught marketing, organization development, conflict management, social research, and socio-economic approach to management. Heorhiadi has consulted in academia, healthcare, non-profit sector and government. With John Conbere, she has co-authored a number of articles on SEAM and organizational change.

Contents

Chapter 1

What Is Different About SEAM: A Quick Peek

When learning and trying to understand new information, people tend to parallel this new information with what they already know. Thus, very often, the first question people ask is how socio-economic approach to management (SEAM) is different from other change management or consulting approaches. This chapter provides a brief summary of the most important, and sometimes radical, ideas that differentiate SEAM from other disciplines. In later chapters, these concepts are elaborated in more detail.

Socio-economic focus. An efficient workplace must deal with the human side as well as the profit, or economic, side. This is what *socio-economic* is all about. Henri Savall has a nice way to explain this term. He keeps a coin in his pocket and when people ask him about SEAM, he shows them the coin. He first holds it with someone's (depending on the country and coin) profile up, "What do you see here? A human, or socio." Then he turns it and exposes the other side with the value of the coin, "What do you see now? Money or economics. The whole coin is socio-economic. The sides do not work without each other." His point is that one cannot separate the people side, or "socio," from the economic side, or productivity and profit, without creating a distortion. The separation is delusional and only hurts one's understanding of an "organizational coin." The delusion has warped management in the modern workplace. The current mental model of management places much more attention on the economic side rather than on the people side, or as it is frequently called, dismissively, "the soft side." Ironically, focusing only on the economic side leads to a reduction of organizational productivity and profits in the long term.

It is also incorrect to assume that SEAM has two foci — people (socio) and financial results (economic). The focus is one, and it is symbolized by the hyphen in the word "socio-economic." Each provides a different view of the same phenomenon. Linguistically, a hyphen's function is to join two ordinarily separate words into one single word. Therefore, "socio-economic" becomes a single word which represents the only focus of SEAM.

Human potential. The socio-economic focus allows for developing human potential — another cornerstone idea of the socio-economic theory. SEAM is based on the premise that the source of value added in organizations lies in developing human potential. This premise challenges the neo-classical economic theory that emphasizes the role of capital in increasing value added, as well as the Marxist economic theory with its idea that labor is the source of value added. According to the SEAM theory, the way to enrich an organization's profit is to invest in people and grow their potential. When people develop, they become more engaged and more interested in contributing to the organization's well-being. All people have potential and, if they are in the right place, they can add value to an organization.

A different mental model of management. Modern Western organizational management theory is rooted in concepts developed during the beginnings of the Industrial Revolution in the late 1800s and early 1900s, and is shaped by a series of thought leaders of that time. More than a century later, this theory still remains the dominant mental model of management of the great majority of leaders in the Western world. This mental model includes a set of flawed beliefs about the human nature, work, and workplace. According to this model, employees are a commodity, human capital, which in the time of financial crisis should be disposed of. Savall and his colleagues named this mental model the Taylorism, Fayolism, Weberism (TFW) virus. This concept is so radical that it gets the most pushback from many managers and is the least understood. The concept challenges the way modern organizations are being managed.

The role of management. One of the goals of SEAM is to change how people manage. While it may be politically incorrect to say this about management, it is necessary to identify that the cause of many organizational problems is poor management. Often, people are promoted to managerial positions based on their technical knowledge or skills. However, being a good professional does not automatically make people good managers, as knowing and managing a business process is different from managing people. Some managers, or supervisors, do not have any managerial training or knowledge of management tools, and sometimes they may have little to no training in interpersonal communication and conflict management. Many managers are taught some very poor habits, and/or they pick these habits up through the examples of management they see around them.

Poor management is not the fault of the individual managers; it is both a failure of an organizational system and the result of the dominant mental model of management. Therefore, during the SEAM intervention in an organization, managers are trained and sometimes to retrained, so they are effective in their role of steering people toward organizational strategic goals.

Changing the system vs. changing individuals. Frequently, when there is a problem in an organization, the tendency is to blame individuals. However, an organization is a system and if something does not work, then the system becomes unhealthy. The unhealthy system is the problem, so blaming individuals will not fix the organizational system. In current business practice, blaming employees for problems is quite common. Blaming is also unethical because it is the unhealthy system's dysfunctions that make employees less effective. Organizational problems and dysfunctions are what evaporate people's energy. Usually, most employees try to do their best and they are willing to contribute to the success of their organizations. SEAM's focus is on fixing the system without attaching the blame for problems to individuals.

Whole system intervention. SEAM intervention deals with whole system change. The intervention starts with the top leaders and cascades down through the organization to reach all parts of the organization. In the first year of a typical SEAM intervention, the leaders and two to three silos (depending on the size) are part of the intervention. Each year, more silos are added, until the whole organization has been involved in SEAM. The systemic nature of SEAM pertains not only to intervening with the whole organizational system but also in the way the intervention is carried out. The intervention is conducted by a team of intervener-researchers, who bring much experience and expertise to shape each intervention. The interaction of two systems — the organization itself and the external consulting team — works better than when a single consultant tries to change an organization.

Hidden costs analysis. While a SEAM intervention may look like other organization development and change interventions, one of the biggest differences is calculating hidden costs, or in other words, attaching a financial figure to things that do not work. Knowing that there are some problems in an organization is not a big surprise, yet seeing the value of what the organization loses due to dysfunctions can be shocking. To help the reader understand what amount of loss the organization deals with, it is sufficient to say that the average amount of hidden costs for an average organization would be more than $20,000 per employee per year. In high-tech companies or heavy-duty manufacturing, this number may rise to $80,000 per employee per year. One can do the math and by multiplying this number with the number of employees, it is easy to see how much a certain organization loses annually.

Information about hidden costs can benefit the organization in two ways. First, when employees, and especially leaders, see the numbers, they are more eager to invest time and effort into resolving the most expensive and risk-generating issues. Second, hidden costs analysis provides leaders with additional information, which they usually do not have when making decisions. The Institut de socio-économie des entreprises et des organisations (ISEOR) research supported Savall's claim that modern accounting does not measure around 40% of what happens financially in an organization. This loss is the result of hidden costs. For an organization to be efficient and stay competitive in the market, leaders need accurate and full information for decision-making. Calculating hidden costs fills the gap between traditional accounting and financial reality in which the organization operates.

The timing of the intervention. When talking about the timing of SEAM interventions, it is important to mention two aspects — pace and duration. In terms of duration, SEAM looks for an organization's commitment to the process for at least a year. While simple changes from the intervention can be seen immediately, the most important and lasting changes begin to become obvious by the end of the first year. Each year of the intervention, the organization sees a higher return on investment. By the end of the third year, the socio-economic mental model has rooted, the organizational culture changed, managers know how to manage well, all of which keep changes in place without needing the interveners' support. The organizational system has healed and is now healthy.

The pace of the intervention is very deliberate, the meetings of interveners-researchers and actors involved in the intervention happen monthly. When it comes to serious changes, there is no rush. A SEAM intervention is not a sprint. It can be compared with a marathon in terms of the distribution of time and effort. Setting a reasonable pace is very important in both organizational change and distance running. In both, the success is measured in the end. The SEAM interveners often must slow down employees, so they do not jump to the "quick fix" of organizational problems before they understand the root causes of the problems. The intervention process is designed thoroughly and each step of the process has its logic. The pace of an intervention helps in maintaining this logical flow toward creating sustainable change.

Actors. To recognize the importance of every person within an organization, instead of using the word "employees," SEAM calls all people in an organization "actors." The term "actors" comes from the European sociology and has the implication that employees in different positions, with different professions are equally important for the success of the organization. One's position does not make the person more important or less important. All actors play some role in the organizational drama and are necessary for an organization to succeed.

Intervener-researcher. SEAM practitioners are trained to be "intervener-researchers," which is, in a way, similar to what in the US is called scholar-practitioners. The intervener-researchers conduct interventions in organizations, and the data collected and analyzed through the intervention process are added to the research database of ISEOR.

Every SEAM intervention conducted by ISEOR and its members since 1973 has served as a research case study that helped to validate and improve the socio-economic theory. The theory shaped the intervention process, or practice, and practice contributed to the theory's robustness. In this way, the gap between practice and theory is bridged. Over 1,800 interventions in different types of organizations, industries, and countries helped to adapt and enrich the socio-economic theory and create quite a unique 40-plus-year-old database of change interventions. In addition, a SEAM contract discloses the intention to conduct research and publish its results. The organization may choose to identify itself in the published research or stay anonymous.

The difference between intervener-researchers and scholar-practitioners is that the latter do not have a common practice for the collection of data about organizations that receive consulting services, do not have a centralized site for storing and analyzing the research data, and usually do not have the research and publication intent included in the contract.

Social responsibility. Capitalism can be beneficial or destructive for nations. Capitalism that has few guidelines or restrictions allows the rich to dominate, to compound their riches, while the people, who do the work, receive a minimal reward for their labor. "Socially responsible capitalism" balances the rewards of capitalism so that benefits of work are shared by owners, leaders, and workers. In addition, there is recognition that organizations have a duty to serve the common good as well as owners or stockholders. In socio-economic theory, respect for each individual person goes hand in hand with the effort to increase profits.

Summary

SEAM is based on several concepts that radically differ from mainstream economic and management beliefs about effective and profitable organizations.

- Human potential is the sustainable source of value added in the workplace.
- There are some serious flaws in the dominant mental model of management in Western societies, which causes poor performance of organizations.

- Poor organizational performance is the product of organizational dysfunctions and hidden costs. The average hidden costs exceed $20,000 per employee per year.
- The most effective organizational change involves the whole system and begins with leaders.
- Consultants, who help organizations to improve performance, should also be researchers contributing to academic knowledge. Thereby intervener-researchers bridge the common gap between theory and practice.
- Organizations have a duty to society as well as to owners and share-holders, a responsibility that can lead to socially responsible capitalism.

Chapter 2

The Core SEAM Concepts

The socio-economic approach to management (SEAM) is an umbrella for the socio-economic theory, the SEAM change intervention, and SEAM management tools and tactics. These three elements are much intertwined — the theory feeds the practice, which in turn is based on theory. The tools are part of practice, yet the underlying philosophy behind the management tools is rooted in the theory. This chapter describes the most important concepts of the socio-economic theory that shape the SEAM practice.

The SEAM Four-Leaf Clover

The four-leaf clover is a metaphorical image that reflects a core tenet of SEAM (see Figure 2.1). Every organization has structures and behaviors. Structures — processes, rules, organization charts, and buildings — are the things that shape the work. Behaviors are what actors do. The four-leaf clover is an illustration of what happens in an organization. The structures and actors' behaviors interact with and influence each other and make the organization work, or function. The organization is supposed to perform many different functions, but when the functions do not work well, they turn into dysfunctions. Consequently, anything that does not work has a cost, or a waste, thus dysfunctions create hidden costs. What happens in the four petals of the clover, i.e. shapes economic

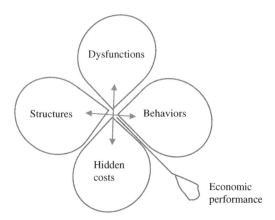

Figure 2.1.   The SEAM four-leaf clover.

performance. The more the dysfunctions, the poorer the economic performance.

Most modern organizations, in their effort to improve their effectiveness, typically focus on changing the structures and/or behaviors. Examples in changing structures are changing the organizational chart, buying new equipment, implementing software, or IT systems. Changes in behaviors may take forms of training employees, implementing new incentives or restrictions, or anything that aims at changing people's behavior. The SEAM theory posits that such direct changes in the workplace are not sustainable and often fail.

There are two reasons these direct changes fail. One reason is that people usually resist when change is forced or imposed upon them. The improvement of processes (structure) may be necessary but when workers do not believe they have any say in the changes, they might resist these changes. Resistance may take different forms: workers may not comply with orders; they may stop caring, rebel, quit, or do anything to act out their displeasure. An example of this failure can be seen in the attempts to implement Lean in the US. Most often, Lean efforts do not sustain in the long term.

The other reason that change fails is because while changing structures or processes, an organization may forget about the needs of those who operate these structures and processes. In other words, the human side of the workplace is ignored. For instance, people need to be heard and feel respected. At the same time, in many workplaces, leaders believe that only leaders know enough to make changes, including how to fix problems in the workplace. This tacit belief is rarely challenged even though the premise is insulting to the intelligence and ability of workers. If workers were respected, they would be part of any attempt to correct problems in the workplace. Usually, the workers on the floor are the ones who know the details of the problem and the possible solutions.

Changing structures can lead to firing people. There many euphemisms to cover up the act of firing workers, such as laying people off, letting people go, "down-sizing" or even "right-sizing" the organization. When changing structures leads to firing actors, the fear of losing one's job and income triggers resistance to change. Workers who are not fired, may have survivor's guilt, may feel unsafe, and lose trust in leadership and organization. This is another example of how not addressing the human side will undermine changes in structures and behaviors.

According to the SEAM theory, rather than starting with the petals of structures and behaviors, the initial focus has to be on the petals of dysfunctions and hidden costs. Addressing these petals first will lead to a better alignment of structures and behaviors, which in turn will reduce resistance to change and increase economic performance of the organization.

Economic performance. When assessing their effectiveness, many organizations focus only on short-term performance. Savall proposed a concept of overall economic performance, which he defined as a combination of "immediate results," produced in the short term, and "creation of potential," which are actions aimed at creating future economic results. While working to achieve immediate results needed to survive, an organization has to invest strategically in the future through creating potential, both human and organizational. The optimal development means that the organization is viable immediately and is set to grow in the future (see Figure 2.2).

Organizational Dysfunctions

Interactions of organizational structures and actors' behaviors generate organizational functions. Savall described the state of proper and well-performed functions as "ortho-functioning." If functions for any reason do

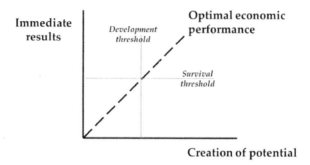

Figure 2.2.   Two axes of an organization's economic performance.

not work properly, they become dysfunctions. Having some dysfunctions is normal, given the need to coordinate various people and processes. Yet, if organizations have many dysfunctions, they become less effective. Organizational dysfunctions evaporate the energy of people and waste the materials and money of an organization. Dysfunctions waste organizational resources at different rates. Sometimes, they act like a dripping faucet, quietly dispersing organizational resources. Sometimes, they act like a waterfall, causing an organizational crisis. The problem with the dysfunctions is not that they cannot be fixed, but rather that people get used to the dysfunctions and begin to believe that there is no other way to work.

To be effective, organizations should have a series of well-functioning areas. All actors need to have good *working conditions*. *Work* processes have to be well *organized* and synchronized. To have synchronized efforts across an organization, the organization needs good *communication* between actors and divisions, good *coordination* of all processes, and *cooperation* among all actors. Actors need to have good knowledge and skills to perform their work, in other words, actors need good *training*. Having the right information (communication), training, and organized work processes helps actors to *manage* their *time*. All of the above facilitate the *implementation* of organizational *strategy* and achieving strategic goals and mission. Therefore, there are six major organizational functions, or areas, in which dysfunction may happen (see Table 2.1).

Table 2.1.   Six areas of dysfunctions and their descriptions.

Area of dysfunctions	Description
Work conditions	This category includes the layout of the work space, equipment and supplies, security, work schedules and hours, and workplace climate.
Work organization	This category includes all aspects of how work processes are organized, e.g., how tasks are distributed among actors, the level of actors' autonomy, actors' work load, organization's and industry regulations, and organizational chart.
Communication–coordination–cooperation, or 3Cs	This category includes all possible aspects of communication within the organization and outside of it, such as with customers and partners. This category also includes the extent to which groups within the organization work collaboratively and synchronically.
Time management	This category includes anything that impacts use of time in the workplace, the effectiveness of planning and scheduling, the timeliness of tasks carried out, and disturbances that hurt timeliness of processes.
Integrated training	This category includes aspects of training that are needed to on-board and develop actors, as well as the analysis of training needs.
Implementation of strategy	This category includes any issues of strategic planning, communications about strategic plans, all tools that aid in carrying out a strategic plan, including budgeting, information systems, personnel management, and management style.

Hidden Costs

The term "hidden costs" refers to the fact that the costs are not obvious, they stay under the radar of traditional accounting practices and do not show directly on financial statements of organizations. While these costs are hidden, they are very real. The Institut de socio-économie des entreprises et des organizations (ISEOR) research showed that the average hidden cost exceeds $20,000 per employee per year. The amount of hidden costs depends on the organization, industry, and other factors. Yet, the bigger and more technologically advanced an organization is, the more the hidden costs occur in the organization.

Indicators of hidden costs. Although hidden costs do not show on the organization's financial sheets, they can be tracked through quantifiable symptoms or indicators. There are five indicators of the hidden costs:

- Absenteeism
- Occupational injuries and diseases
- Staff turnover
- Poor quality
- Reduced productivity

These indicators can be found in the organization's records. "Absenteeism," "occupational injuries and diseases," and "staff turnover" are self-explanatory. "Poor quality" refers to the products that are not good enough to sell for the regular price, so either they are thrown away or discounted. "Reduced productivity" refers to a lower volume of production, or services provided, comparatively with what the organization can produce or provide.

Categories of hidden costs. It is important to note that hidden costs are not always hard cash, and identifying and reducing them will not release money that can go back into the organization's financial circulation. Hidden costs may take different forms, all of which will lead to negative financial consequences for the organization. There are six categories of hidden costs, four of which represent waste in the present time and the other two categories of hidden costs refer to waste in the future.

Table 2.2 shows the categories of hidden costs and their descriptions. We included English and French terms to help readers, who have read work of Savall and his colleagues, navigate between the terms. We made these changes to help the American audience understand the categories more easily. For instance, the French use of "overtime" refers to the extra time that is wasted due to a dysfunction. For an American, "overtime" refers to the higher pay hourly workers receive for working beyond 40 h per week.

Table 2.2. Description of categories of hidden costs.

| Time frame | Category of hidden costs | | Description |
	English term	French term	
Financial consequences are measured "in the present"	Wasted money	Overconsumption	Financial value of resources consumed due to dysfunctions
	Wasted time	Overtime	The value of wasted time due to dysfunctions
	Overpaying for a shift in function	Excess salary	Paying someone to do the work that ought to be done by someone with a lower qualifications or salary
	Missed productivity	Non-production	Loss of productivity caused by dysfunctions
Possible financial consequences are estimated "in the future"	Not developing potential	Non-creation of potential	Failure to prepare employees and organization for work in the future
	Risks	Risks	Failure to avoid potential problems

Root Causes of Dysfunctions

An organization may have hundreds or thousands of dysfunctions. All these dysfunctions are caused by just a few major organizational problems, the root causes of dysfunctions. To illustrate the root causes, we use the ISEOR's image of a causal tree, which is shown in Figure 2.3.

In the image of the tree, the leaves represent dysfunctions, the berries represent hidden costs, and the twigs and branches represent the alleged causes of the dysfunctions. The natural organizational instinct is to deal with leaves and berries because they are visible. However, usually the leaves and berries are symptoms of deeper underlying problems, which are harder to recognize and also take more effort and time to fix. If the organization removes leaves and berries, in the short term, it may look like the organization

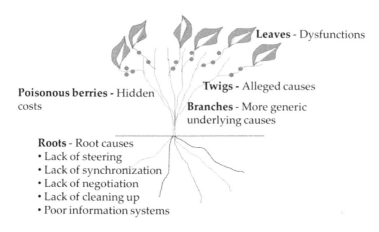

Figure 2.3.   The five root causes of organizational dysfunctions.

fixed the problems. In the long term, new leaves and poisonous berries grow again, and new dysfunctions and hidden costs reoccur. Rather than dealing with symptoms, it is important to identify and deal with the root problems. Finding and eradicating the root problems will help to create the right solution for the problem that will work and sustain.

Lack of steering. This is the primary root cause of many dysfunctions. Steering includes not only setting organizational strategic goals, but also aligning people with resources and directing people toward achieving those goals. Thus, steering is both leading and managing and is the primary task of any leader and/or manager. Top leaders steer an organizational ship; managers and supervisors steer their division. When actors in an organization are not sure about the direction of their organization or how their work fits into that direction, they are less effective and engaged. Lack of steering can happen at any level — from front-line supervisor to the CEO and Board of Directors.

Lack of synchronization. This refers to the failure to coordinate the organizational processes and align actors' efforts in achieving organizational goals. As a result, while individually employees or some parts of the organization may work very hard, their work is not synchronized with other parts of the organization, and collectively the organization is not efficient. A bigger problem than reduced efficiency, however, is turf wars in which actors in different silos fight for organizational resources. Turf wars waste the organization's energy, disorient employees, and weaken organizational strategy.

Lack of cleaning up. This occurs when a change is made, and the old instructions, or rules, or practices that have been made obsolete are not eliminated. Instead, there is a growing hodgepodge of work practices that make less and less sense. We call this phenomenon "organizational hoarding," which is accumulating different policies, procedures, rules, rituals, or routines, without timely reviewing, changing, and discarding the ones that are outdated. Organizational hoarding can be intentional and unintentional. With intentional hoarding, an organization is reluctant to discard anything in case something might be needed in the future or because the organization has followed the policy for years. Unintentional hoarding happens when the organization does not have or make time to review the old processes. As a result, different parts of an organization live by different rules, some of which might be contradictory.

One example of lack of cleaning up is when actors are asked to do more work without removing any tasks of the original workload. There is no way people can do more and more without reducing quality and/or burning out. Yet, some people seem to believe this continual loading of work is possible. We call this phenomenon magical thinking, which is the belief that somehow, magically, the overburdened worker will be able to excel, simply because the manager has ordered this to happen. For more on magical thinking, see Chapter 6.

Poor information systems. This means that actors do not get the information they need to do their work well. Examples of poor information systems can be inefficient computer systems, managers who do not tell subordinates the information needed to excel, the departments that do not share information with each other, or the employees at the bottom of the hierarchy who are afraid to tell superiors something due to the fear of being punished. As a result, employees do not have the right information to make wise decisions and to work well.

In the ISEOR version of root causes, poor information systems are titled HISOFIS — Humanly Integrated and Stimulating Operational and Functional Information Systems. The term in a way is very self-explanatory and logical. For information to be useful, it must be understood by people (humanly integrated) and acted upon (has to lead to, or stimulate, some actions). Any information that is not easily available and usable is dysfunctional and/or leads to other dysfunctions. Thus, lack of HISOFIS is one of the root causes of organization problems. In summary, to work effectively, an organization needs to have information systems that are humanly usable, integrated, and yield data that stimulates people to action.

Lack of negotiation. According to the socio-economic theory, there will always be conflict between actors in organizations. Conflict is inevitable because the organization and each individual have different needs. Here are some examples: the organization may want more profit and the employee may want time for family; managers may want employees to follow certain procedures and employees may become bored by repetitive processes; managers may not listen well to the employees and employees may want their ideas to be heard. In each case, if the conflict is not named and discussed, i.e., negotiated, the conflict will remain unresolved and will have the potential to cause dysfunctions and de-motivate employees. Negotiation is a productive and respectful means of resolving these conflicts. Without negotiation, it is hard to align resources and people, coordinate work processes, and achieve the optimal organizational economic and human performance.

In many organizations, the idea of negotiating tends to be outside of the view of what is acceptable. The exception, perhaps, is negotiating salary and benefits upon being hired, but other than that, often workers believe that they cannot negotiate and instead should comply. This belief is part of the existing dominant mental model of management (the Taylorism, Fayolism, Weberism (TFW) virus), according to which, workers are supposed to be always obedient and do not try to argue about management decisions. The tacit message is that workers' insights and needs are irrelevant in the bigger scope of organizational goals. When workers have to squash their needs, insights, or hopes, they lose some of their enthusiasm, which reduces their engagement and ability to reach their potential. When all actors of an organization do not reach their potential, the organization also loses that energy and loses the potential for advancing the organization's interests.

Interrelationship of root causes. Like tree roots, the root causes of dysfunctions can be entangled. For example, poor steering may lead to a lack of synchronization and alignment among the different parts of an organization. Lack of clean-up leads to having different rules and policies in different parts of organization, which also may exacerbate the lack of synchronization. Poor information systems can be the result of poor steering and also add to lack of synchronization. In a working system, causes may not always be discrete. Nonetheless, being able to recognize the root causes of dysfunctions is invaluable when diagnosing an organization.

Human Potential

Socio-economic theory posits that the only way to have significant and sustainable organizational growth is by developing human potential. That is the economic importance of human potential. Classical economic theory begins with the assumption that capital is the source of development of value. One can add financial resources to an organization and it will have more financial value. The financial resources by themselves do not cause the organization to grow in value, other than having a larger bank account — because money itself does not cause growth. Marxist economics begins with the assumption that labor is the source of the development of value, but more workers alone does not increase value as well.

Everyone has potential. Releasing this potential increases employee contribution to the organization, which in turn increases the organization's value. The increase of employee contribution may result from using people's untapped skills, freeing people from barriers that prevent them to use those skills, or tapping into people's talents and passion. In Gallup poll terms, people become engaged.

Here is an example of two imaginary workplaces. In workplace A, actors drag themselves to work every morning to do what they are told to do. Actors are supposed to be obedient and follow the rules strictly. There is not much room for autonomy, as they are being continuously micromanaged. There is not much room for creativity either, as the actors learned not to take risks. If something does not go well, for any reason, their manager blames them for the error, and uses some form of punishment "to improve their performance." The work does not bring joy, except perhaps, when the actors are paid. By the end of the day, actors feel drained physically and emotionally and have neither energy nor desire to dream about how to grow or improve their organization. Managers in this workplace neither use the actors' abilities well nor nurture the actors' talents and thus they did not tap into actors' potential.

In workplace B, actors come to work, excited. They are passionate about their work, they do it well, and their manager recognizes this. They feel autonomous enough to do their tasks, and often have creative ideas about how to improve and grow the organization. On occasions when those ideas do not work out, their managers tell them that errors are just learning opportunities. Then the actors collectively decide how to resolve the problem. All actors know how their individual efforts contribute to the bigger organizational mission. This workplace has tapped human potential, which will result in the organization's competitive edge, increased value, and sustainable growth in the long term.

It is easy to see many differences between the two imagined workplaces. Yet, one difference that is very important is the underlying assumption about the source of errors. In workplace A, the source of error is the actor, and the assumption is that the actor could have avoided the error. In workplace B, the assumption is that the actors try to do their work well; the source of errors is the broken or inefficient organization. Often, it may look like the error is the fault of the employee, yet in reality, the error is the result of organizational dysfunctions. For example, the employee did not have the right training to work well, or did not have the right information, or was not steered well by managers, or was asked to do more tasks than is possible, none of which is a sign of the actor's deliberate intention to not do work well.

Socially, there is an ethical aspect to the belief in the importance of human potential. People deserve the opportunity to develop. Hiring an actor does not give an organization the right to put the person in an emotional and intellectual cage, working to earn money for owners at the price of developing human potential. The sources of this belief are from the economic theorists Germán Bernácer and François Perroux, and the belief is in harmony with the radical Christian teachings of Popes John XXIII and Francis.

The concept of developing human potential permeates the socio-economic theory. The need to invest in human potential shapes the SEAM change intervention, in which the goal is healing the system without blaming the individual. The concept of human potential is also reflected in the

SEAM management tools, that are designed not to control and punish employees, but rather to teach managers how to manage more effectively. It is important for organizations to understand that developing human potential is the only economically viable way to sustain change and development, and the only ethically responsible way to treat people.

The TFW Virus

While working on his socio-economic approach to management and testing it in organizations, Savall noticed that most organizations had a gap between work design and execution, hyperbolized work specialization, and numerous regulations that were designed to shape and control human behavior. He realized that the way the organizations were designed, as well as assumptions about management, were rooted in earlier management theories. Later, he created a metaphor to describe those assumptions and named it the Taylorism, Fayolism, Weberism virus, or the TFW virus.

The metaphor was named after Taylor, Fayol, and Weber because these three men heavily influenced the theory of management at the beginning of the 20th century. Frederick W. Taylor (1856–1915) was an American engineer who developed the idea of scientific management. He studied ways to obtain the maximum efficiency in work, one of which to him, was the separation between the design and execution of work. Henri Fayol (1841–1925), a French engineer, is credited for establishing much of the theory of business administration. He argued for the hierarchical chain of command and thus stressed the importance of order. Fayol claimed that the authority and responsibility of managers gave them the right to expect obedience from the subordinates. Max Weber (1864–1920) was a German sociologist who posited that the ideal organizational model is bureaucracy that is based on the definition of rules, which are then respected and followed by subjects.

Individually, Taylor, Fayol, and Weber worked to improve the efficiency of the workplace and, to some extent at least, to improve the condition of workers. Collectively, the ideas of Taylor, Fayol, and Weber shaped the modern theory of management that is still being taught in business schools in North America and Europe. TFW ideas have become the accepted assumptions about management not only for most managers, but also for those who are being managed, workers. There is some debate about whether the modern view of the TFW theories is accurate or has been misinterpreted, but that is not the point. The point is that modern business and management were shaped by the theories of Taylor, Fayol, and Weber more than a century ago. The TFW ideas, while being relevant in the time of their founders, do not take into account changes in the business and ecological environments, changes in technology and education, and different people's expectations of professional and personal lives. Thus, the TFW ideas cannot possibly address the needs of modern people, time, and environment; moreover, they are destructive to the human soul.

First, we need to define some terms. A set of beliefs and assumptions about how some things work and interrelate form a "mental model," or in other terms a "frame of reference," or a "paradigm." The TFW virus is a metaphor to describe the mental model of modern management and organizational concepts. The TFW virus mental model includes the set of beliefs about the nature of people, work, and workplace, as they pertain to organizations.

TFW assumption about human nature. From the TFW perspective, the economic human being is rational. "Rational" derives from the Latin word "rationalis," which means reasonable or logical. Therefore, a rational human being is supposed to work based on logic, sound judgment, or good sense. The workplace is not the place for emotions, feelings, or whims. Actors should leave their personal problems at the door and work-related problems should not be influenced by actors' moods.

TFW beliefs about work. The core assumption about the rational nature of human beings shapes two beliefs about work. The first belief is about losing one's individuality and becoming an organizational resource. When people are hired, by contract, they must be obedient, work for the good of the organization, and follow the workplace rules. In other words, with a work contract, an employee becomes a commodity, or human capital, to be used for the gain of owners. One could argue that, in the end, this means that employees sell their independence, and thus a piece of their soul, for the privilege of being paid.

The second belief is about the different natures of life at work and life at home. When coming to work, employees should leave part of their self, e.g., their emotions, feelings, and desires, at home and turn into rational, emotionless entities. Yes, employees have feelings, but dealing with feelings is often seen as a nuisance rather than the inevitable outcome of dealing with a person. An echo of this second belief could be found in modern discussions about the topic of work–life balance. While the idea of work–life balance is admirable, it carries in its heart the flawed assumption that work and life are different and there should be time for each. The term, work–life balance, may be a Freudian slip that reveals the hidden bias of the modern workplace: work is not a part of life — working is the alternative to living. The SEAM approach is that work is a part of life, not an alternative to life.

TFW beliefs about work and the workplace. The beliefs about the nature of human beings and work shape the beliefs about how the workplace should be designed. According to the TFW virus, the effective workplace should have the following features:

Hyper-specialization. Division of labor and specialization were a product of the beginning of the industrialization era in pursuit of increasing factory productivity and workers' output. What used to be a craft job of one worker was divided into many specialized jobs for many different workers. Each worker had to be specialized in a small task rather than capable of performing all of the tasks in a complex production process. For manufacturing of that era, division of labor and specialization were justified, as they led to lower costs, higher efficiencies, and greater productivity. For the worker though, this meant concentrating on more narrow and isolated parts of the job.

At its worst, monotonous repetition of the same small tasks may lead to boredom, loss of interest in work, and mental dullness. Such work kills the initiative, creativity, and desire to learn. Focusing only on a small part of the product reduces the role of workers in the production process and makes it harder to take pride in the final result. The worker is no longer a craftsman, but an animate cog in the organizational machine. While historically specialization is associated with manufacturing assembly lines, hyper-specialization can be seen in different industries and forms now, for instance, in the fields of knowledge or information. Hyper-specialization may look economically efficient in short term, but eventually it reduces workers' job satisfaction, engagement, and involvement in growing the value of the organization.

Separation. Originally, this concept was about separating work design and work execution. According to the TFW virus, workers were not clever enough to participate in the design process. Only educated people like engineers or managers could do the design process. The "smarter" leaders also should fix any problems that arise in the workplace. Separation can be reflected in other areas: separating the thinkers from the doers, the "noble" tasks from the "menial" tasks, the areas and perks for managers from areas for workers, and separating life at work from life at home.

People must be submissive to the organization's needs. The premise is that the purpose of business is to make a profit. Thus, the work process is primary and the needs of the person are subordinate to profit. The core TFW assumption about the rational nature of people leads to the idea that people can and should be submissive to the organization's needs. They sold their labor to the organization, therefore they are supposed to be obedient and obey their management and organizational rules. The belief about submissiveness is the most corrupting to the human soul because the belief allows the organization to treat workers as human capital, a commodity that can be disposed whenever it is perceived that workers do not obey or for the purpose of increasing short-term profits for the organization.

The consequences of the TFW virus. Any mental model, even though it is usually invisible, produces visible human behaviors and outcomes. The consequences of the TFW virus are the fractured workplace, heartless processes, depersonalization, and elitism, all of which hurt people and productivity.

The workplace is fractured. The workplace is broken into many different parts. There is an obvious geographical division that can be between departments and different organizational silos. There is also social division that can be seen among generations, professions, genders, ranks, groups, "us and them," and other social groups. The fractured workplace hurts people, hurts productivity, and reduces organizational effectiveness. Human trust is weakened, cooperation is undercut, communication is broken, joy is minimal, and satisfaction, even if present, does not come from a deep sense of participating in meaningful work.

Heartless processes. When people in the workplace are seen as human capital, which is disposable when no longer needed, the result is heartless processes. The needs of the organization are more important than the needs of the individual. Rules must be obeyed and "if we let one person do this, we have to let everyone do it." Reason and compassion go out the door in favor of conformity and organizational convenience. Here is an example of a heartless process. One company was very strict about following its HR policies. An employee's father was slowly dying of cancer, and finally he was put into hospice care. The employee had used up all his sick leave for the year. He stayed out of work in the last few days of his father's life, caring for him in hospice. Nevertheless, the employee was "written up" for his absence, which meant he could get no pay raise and no promotion for the next 6 months. Rules were valued more than compassion. The process was heartless.

In large organizations, the sense of the organization, as an entity, creates a tremendous pressure to comply with the organizational norms, and concern for individuals can easily be lost. The result is that individuals become cogs in the machine, rather than autonomous creative human beings who deserve respect and care.

Depersonalization. Separation and heartless processes slowly lead to a loss of one's sense of self, or depersonalization. This loss of one's sense of self is the opposite of self-actualization, and results in diminishing the person, the withering of the human soul. People lose interest in their work, and lose hope that change is possible. They become disengaged at work, and the disengagement can carry over to the rest of life.

Elitism. The TFW virus fosters elitism, the belief that some individuals are superior to others. The idea of elitism was described by Weber in *The Protestant Ethic and the Spirit of Capitalism*, in 1930. Weber posited that Puritan Protestantism led to the belief that if one is successful, one must be favored by God, otherwise God would not allow the person to be successful. By this belief, to be successful in business means that one is morally and spiritually superior.

Today, elitism is still ingrained in the modern workplace, and superiority is demonstrated by rank in the organization. To be higher on an organizational ladder implicitly means to be better, superior to those who are below. Some people truly believe that they are actually superior to others, and so they deserve their perks and sometimes exorbitant salaries.

People who believe they are superior also believe that they must be treated differently from others. "Superiors" want to preserve and reinforce their privileged place by creating laws, rules, and traditions that serve to protect their privileged place. The "superior" mindset uses the following logic: Status comes with certain attributes and symbols, which are deserved and important. It is acceptable for leaders to be self-serving. The self-justification of differences helps to secure the status of those higher in the hierarchy. This mindset is vividly seen in some executives' salaries, which can reach tens of millions of dollars a year. Their earnings can be 500–2,000 times the earnings of someone at the bottom of the hierarchy, which are justified with reasons like the need to be competitive for the best leaders. However, the logic of self-justification dances around reason, allowing greed to flourish.

Blindness. The four phenomena described above are accepted without any reservations as an inevitable part of work. People stop seeing the damage caused by the TFW virus mental model and become blind to what happens in front of them every day.

The idea of blindness is not new. People in organizations become blind to unpleasant things and pretend those things do not exist. Chris Argyris, an American business and organization development theorist, called these phenomena "organizational defensive routines." To maintain their pretense, or delusion, people use "fancy footwork," a mechanism to explain away any inconsistencies between what people say and what they do. Fancy footwork consists either of denying that the inconsistencies exist, or placing the blame on other people.

Figure 2.4 is the visual representation of the TFW virus.

It is possible to use an example of a virus in a human body to understand how the TFW virus works. A real virus is a small infectious agent that replicates only inside the living cells of other organisms. The virus lives in a host cell and eventually leads to the death of the host cell. Disease-bearing viruses weaken an immune system, which in turn limit the body's ability to resist stress and/or environmental impact. The TFW virus lives in the human mind and replicates through teachings about management. The TFW virus infects organizations, lowers the organization's "immunity," and hurts organizational health through dysfunctions and hidden costs. When an organization is in good condition the disease may be dormant; in a time of stress or crisis, the symptoms of the disease are very visible: massive layoffs and getting rid of expensive human "commodities"

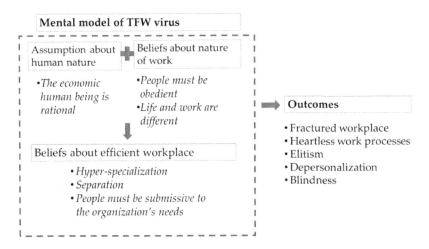

Figure 2.4.   The outcome of the TFW virus is the unhealthy workplace.

(heartless processes), offering golden parachutes to failed leaders (elitism), turf wars between silos that hurt organizational effectiveness (fractured workplace), the total disregard and disrespect of employees' insights and needs (depersonalization), and followed up by a pretense that all this is normal (blindness).

The TFW virus has corrupted the understanding of work and management in Western societies. The assumptions in the mental model have become the dominant ideology of modern business and management. Socio-Economic theory was developed as an antidote to the TFW virus. SEAM becomes a remedy to help integrate the socio and economic aspects of work, reduce separation and brokenness, increase employee involvement in the fate of the organization, restore the meaning of work, and bring joy into the workplace. In other words, SEAM is designed to heal the workplace and modern organizations.

Summary

The essence of how an organization works is represented by the concept of the four-leaf clover. Every organization has structures and behaviors, and if they are not working well, they cause dysfunctions. Dysfunctions cause hidden costs. The most effective way to change an organization is to work backward. Identifying dysfunctions and calculating hidden costs help leaders to look beyond symptoms to the root causes of the dysfunctions. Information about root causes pushes actors to improve organizational structures through collective work across silos and levels of rank to reduce the dysfunctions and hidden costs.

Reducing hidden costs allows organizations to release resources that can be invested in developing human potential and organizational effectiveness. Developing human potential is not only ethical and good for people, but it is the only economically viable way to sustain organizational development and well-being.

The TFW virus is the flawed mental model of management rooted in the beginning of the industrialization era, and it has a destructive influence on individuals and organizations. The TFW virus is a metaphor to describe the set of beliefs about human nature, work, and workplace. Addressing the infected assumptions about people and work will help modern organizations flourish.

Chapter 3

The SEAM Intervention

Before describing the actual process of implementing the socio-economic approach to management (SEAM) in organizations, it is important to introduce two new concepts that serve as the theoretical foundation of how SEAM is implemented in the workplace — "SEAM trihedron" and "Horivert" process.

The SEAM Trihedron

The SEAM change intervention is a combination of three simultaneous processes and thus has three foci: (a) improvement process, (b) teaching leaders and managers about the socio-economic management and the SEAM management tools, and (c) coaching leaders through the implementation of organizational changes. Visually, these three foci are represented by the three axes of the process and this is why the change process, in SEAM jargon, is called the trihedron (Figure 3.1).

The improvement process. The improvement process begins with a diagnostic phase, which comprises analyzing organizational dysfunctions and calculating hidden costs. After identifying problems, actors choose projects for improvement and begin work on their implementation. Actors from a division that is going through the SEAM intervention are involved in all stages of the change process — from the data collection to identifying and prioritizing improvement projects. See Figure 3.2 for the detailed steps of the SEAM improvement process.

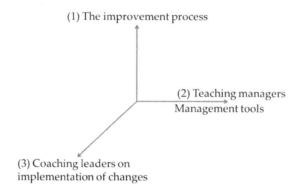

Figure 3.1. The SEAM trihedron (adapted from models by ISEOR).

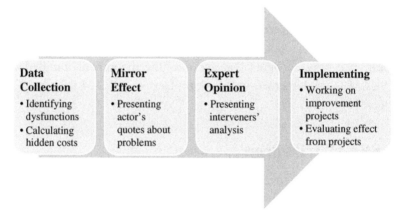

Figure 3.2. The intervention axis of the SEAM trihedron with steps.

The improvement process is similar to Lewin's classic action research. A consultant gathers data from employees, analyzes the data, feeds findings back to employees, and assists them in solving organizational problems. However, there are some elements that differentiate SEAM from other change interventions. First, a diagnostic phase involves calculating hidden costs, which is assessing financial losses due to dysfunction. When actors see how expensive some dysfunctions are, they are motivated to invest time and energy in fixing them.

The second difference is that feedback to employees is divided in two different sessions — Mirror Effect and Expert Opinion. In the Mirror Effect, the feedback consists of employees' quotes about key dysfunctions and the hidden costs calculated by interveners. During the Expert Opinion, which usually happens a month later, the interveners share their analysis, perspectives, and suggestions of potential improvement projects. Splitting the feedback session into two achieves two important goals. First, this approach allows to separate raw data and data interpretation. Second, having a month between sessions allows the employees to absorb the information, reflect on it for some time, and not rush into a quick fix of symptoms.

At the implementation stage of the SEAM intervention, it is important to evaluate whether the project fixed the original dysfunctions that the project was designed to address. One way to evaluate the effect from the project is to estimate whether the amount of the hidden costs related to the dysfunctions has been reduced. If there is reduction, then the project was successful.

Teaching leaders and managers. Any intervention is not sustainable if people do not understand the purpose of the improvement process and if they do not acquire new knowledge and skills to support changes. Therefore, educating leaders and managers is the second axis of the trihedron. Educating includes teaching about SEAM in general and SEAM management tools in specifics.

The management tools are taught to leaders and mangers at all levels of the organization. Additionally, top leaders are taught the core tenets of socio-economic management. Frequently, mid-level managers and frontline supervisors do not have sufficient (or any) training in supervision. Especially in the fields of academia, healthcare, and other trained professions, actors are promoted from the ranks to become supervisors, with little or no experience or education about supervision or management. Therefore, teaching managers' SEAM management tools increase the quality of management and free the managers to do their important job — managing, or in the SEAM language, steering. While SEAM management tools may seem similar to traditional management tools taught in many business schools, they are based on a different philosophy and have a different focus. See Chapter 4 for more explanation.

Additionally, the SEAM intervener-researchers train a few internal SEAM champions, who understand the principles and process of SEAM. Both teaching and preparing internal interveners play an important role in sustaining the change effort.

Coaching leaders on political and strategic decisions. The third axis pertains to coaching leaders through the process of implementing changes to help leaders align changes with the strategic goals and political environment of the organization. As leaders go through the change process and discover the cost of dysfunctions and what needs to be changed, they need to make some decisions. These decisions are both strategic and political, and they have to be tied to the long-term organization's strategy. The decisions can be grouped in the following clusters:

- *Main goals of the organization.* These decisions involve making and following the strategic goals of the organization. Leaders need to communicate the goals to actors in an effective manner.
- *Changing the rules of the game.* These decisions involve the explicit and implicit rules for actors' behavior. For instance, if the Mirror Effect session identified destructive organizational habits that impact organizational effectiveness, the next step would be to agree about how actors ought to behave professionally, and to communicate these new "rules of the game."
- *Resources redeployment.* Change in directions may lead to new needs and consequently to conscious revision of resource allocation. The decisions about resources redeployment are needed to support the reduction of hidden costs and development of human potential.
- *Technological, organizational, and procedural decisions.* As the organization goes through project implementation, leaders may realize the need to make decisions that pertain to organizational technology, structure, and processes.
- *Strategic choices about the product market.* These decisions deal with the position in the market and the need to stay competitive or to grow. These decisions may also be about the use of resources and development of human potential.
- *Choice of management system.* If the intervention disclosed a management system strongly influenced by the Taylorism, Fayolism, Weberism (TFW) virus, then choices about how to manage in a healthier manner will be needed.
- *Strategic development of human resources.* These decisions arise when the organization discovers untapped human potential or

identifies new knowledge and skills that will be needed in the future to sustain organizational growth.

The intervener-researchers help leaders navigate through the changing environment by making informed political and strategic choices. In addition, any coaching to help managers improve their abilities to manage may also be part of what the intervener-researchers offer.

The Horivert Improvement Process

A SEAM intervention is systemic and works with the whole organization. The intervention starts at the top and cascades down to silos until the whole organization is covered. The intervention starts with the top leaders in the organization, or the "horizontal group," followed by work in other parts of the organizations, the "vertical groups." The term "Horivert" highlights the necessity of involvement of both organizational levels — horizontal and vertical, see Figure 3.3.

It is easy to see in Figure 3.3 that some actors are part of both interventions — horizontal and vertical. These are managers, who are heads of various divisions of the organization. These leaders are link pins between the horizontal and vertical groups as they belong both to the leadership

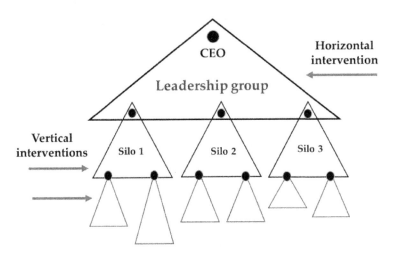

Figure 3.3. The horizontal and vertical components of the "Horivert" intervention.

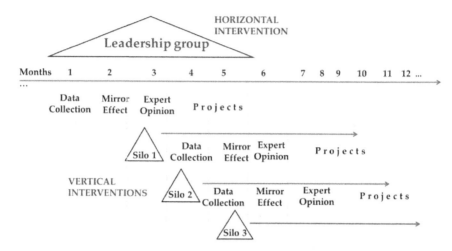

Figure 3.4.   The timeline of the "Horivert" process that starts at the top and cascades down throughout the organization by adding more silos into the process.

group and also manage their divisions. They are involved in improving the work of the leadership group, and they also have to be champions of SEAM in their own divisions. Being involved in the SEAM work on both levels has several positives. First, the division heads are able to communicate to the division members information about SEAM in the horizontal group, so when the turn comes to do SEAM in the division, the actors know the process. Second, leaders, being involved in SEAM on the horizontal level model, change and demonstrate that they are "walking the talk." Third, because leaders are involved in the change process themselves, they send the message to subordinates that it is safe to participate.

SEAM is a system-wide process and the whole organization is involved. However, it is impossible to work with all parts of the organization at once and thus the intervention process is staggered. Figure 3.4 shows how the intervention cascades through the organization.

Diagnostic Phase — Data Collection

The diagnostic phase of the SEAM improvement process begins with data collection by interviewing actors. In the horizontal group, all leaders including the CEO are interviewed about what does not work in the organization in general and in their vertical group specifically. In the vertical groups, the leader(s) are interviewed and at least one-third of the other actors are included in focus groups. The interviews and focus groups are open ended and structured around the six areas of dysfunctions. The intervener-researchers gather information of what does not work as well as it might in the areas of work conditions, work organizations, 3Cs, time management, integrated training, and implementation of strategy. Intervener-researchers' comments are limited to requests for clarification. Often employees are not comfortable talking about negatives, so they shift to describing what works well. However, this is not useful for the organization's diagnosis, so the intervener-researchers have to guide them gently back to talking about dysfunctions.

Once the interviews are completed, the analysis involves identifying comments that pertain to dysfunctions, and clustering them into the right categories of dysfunctions. A list of themes and subthemes of dysfunctions can be found in *Mastering Hidden Costs and Socio-Economic Performance* (Savall & Zardet, 2008, p. 145).

The diagnostic rigor has benefits. After clustering quotes, it is easy to see patterns of organizational problems more easily, which in turn helps discovering the root causes of dysfunctions. At the same time, intervener-researchers need to see the context of the comment to do the accurate diagnostic. For example, if an interviewee said, "My job description is not clear," the quote could be categorized in at least three ways:

a. Work organization → Distribution of tasks → Roles and responsibilities are not clear.
b. Communication–Coordination–Cooperation → Vertical 3Cs → Lack of 3Cs on the part of hierarchical supervisors.
c. Implementation of strategy → Management styles → Managerial staff does not assume its responsibilities.

Each categorization is possible. The implication of each is different. If the issue is that actors' roles are spelled out somewhere, but not shared with actors, then clarifying the roles will suffice. If the issue is that managers are not communicating about roles, perhaps due to lack of time, then the task will be helping the manager prioritize time so there is enough time to steer the employee. If the issue is that managers do not know how to manage, and do not clarify roles to all actors, then a different course is needed. The intervener-researcher has to look at the overall set of interviews and decide which categorization makes the most sense. In other words, the intervener-researcher has to see the quotes in context in order to identify their meaning and make sense of how they fit into the larger picture of the organizational problems.

The Mirror Effect

A month after interviewing actors, the intervener-researchers deliver a feedback session, which is called the Mirror Effect. The term Mirror Effect is self-explanatory — intervener-researchers hold a metaphoric mirror up to an organization. The organization has a chance to look at itself through a different perspective.

All actors of the department are invited to the Mirror Effect session. The feedback is composed only of quotes without any comments or bias on the part of consultants. It goes without saying that the names of the individuals are not mentioned, and to the extent possible individuals are not identified in the comments. Sometimes, when interviewees speak about their manager, it is easy for actors to identify the person, even when the person's name is not used. However, the consultants make the point that the focus of the Mirror Effect is not to blame anyone but rather to name the systemic problems. For example, poor management is not a fault of the person but rather is the result of dysfunctions, such as lack of training, or lack of clear expectations. The consultants emphasize that all people do their best, and the quotes only represent what parts of the system are not working or hindering the efforts of employees. Employees can see that the process is transparent, safe, and fair. All issues are on the table.

Sometimes, during the Mirror Effect session, the actors who are present try to argue about some quotes, saying that they are not true. In those cases, the intervener-researchers may point out that the quotes only show that other people may have a different work experience and thus have different opinions. Socio-economic theory calls this phenomenon contradictory inter-subjectivity, which means that different people have different opinions about an issue.

With other consulting approaches, when consultants analyze the gathered data, they tend to look for trends and if one comment looks like an outlier, it is not included in the analysis. In SEAM, all comments are included. There are several good reasons behind this practice. First, all actors are equal, and each actor deserves to be heard. The person who is the only one to share an opinion has a feeling of being heard; and being heard is important for involving all actors in the change process. Second, sometimes, the opinion of the majority may represent a groupthink, when people become blind to some organizational problems. That one outlier comment may be a beginning of the organization's epiphany. Third, including all actors' comments, no matter how radical or silly they might seem, removes the intervener-researcher from deciding about what is important and what is not. It is the task of the group to decide what deserves their attention.

For example, in one organization during the data collection, many employees focused on work processes, and communication. One actor pointed out that toilet paper in bathrooms was of such poor quality that it was worthless. Usually, one might think that the toilet paper quality is insignificant in the light of major organizational issues, yet we included the comment in the Mirror Effect. At the session, the comment produced a lot of laughter and teasing remarks from the group members. The person who voiced the concern, and who by the way had an epidemiological background, explained that the poor toilet paper is a hazard to a healthy and sanitary workplace. To fast-forward, a week later, all bathrooms were equipped with a better-quality toilet paper, it was an example of instant gratification.

Actors provide comments about what they perceive does not work well. The comments may be the result of actual dysfunctions, or of misunderstanding on the part of the actor. The Mirror Effect allows managers to identify which is which and correct misinformation and misperceptions. Often, the correction happens immediately on the spot. For instance, once someone said that there was no mileage reimbursement for travel during work. This was incorrect, and the supervisor was able to provide the accurate information on the spot.

The Mirror Effect serves several functions. It gets the actors reflecting about what is not working well, which can lead to the beginning of changes that are easy to implement, and to the "unfreezing" of the group for more difficult issues. It clarifies misinformation. Presenting the information back to the actors is a validity check, which lets the intervener-researchers know whether they understood correctly the actors' opinions and concerns.

Assessing hidden costs. In the vertical groups, the Mirror Effect also includes a hidden cost analysis. Hidden costs are not calculated at the horizontal intervention because the senior leadership group is supposed to do strategic tasks, rather than operational tasks; and most of hidden costs happen at the operational level. To calculate hidden costs, the intervener-researchers perform several steps. First, they assess the interviews for signs of dysfunctions and potential hidden costs. Second, they review organizational data, such as records of employee turnover, overtime payments, workplace accidents, or occupational injuries, looking for the indicators of hidden costs. Third, the intervener-researchers interview those actors who can provide information about the occurrence, frequency, and financial implications of the dysfunctions. After the hidden cost interviews, the intervener-researchers are ready to determine the financial losses from dysfunctions.

One of ISEOR's innovations is to calculate the hidden costs by the cost per actor per hour. The method is to calculate the total cost of the non-variable expenses, including the cost of permanent employees, and divide this by the total number of hours worked in the organization in a year. This approach is based on the concept that when an actor wastes time, it is not only the actor's salary that is wasted but also the proportional cost of operating the whole organization in that wasted time. The result is a more accurate representation of loss than merely figuring loss based only on the actor's salary.

Identifying and calculating the hidden costs is like detective work, in which the intervener-researchers tease out the details. For instance, when calculating the hidden costs that result from staff turnover, the intervener-researchers have to look for things like the cost of the time it takes the HR department to hire a new person; expenses involved in hiring, such as advertising; training, and on-boarding costs; lost productivity in the time when the new person is learning a job; and hidden costs from extra work that has been redistributed among the actors who lost a coworker. Note that the intervener-researchers take into account only preventable staff turnover, the ones that resulted from dysfunctions such as employee frustration and low morale. Some turnover is inevitable, such as when people retire or have a spouse who moves to another city.

Calculating different types of hidden costs. Some categories of hidden costs, such as wasted money or lost time, can be calculated with reasonable accuracy (see more on hidden costs categories in Chapter 2). Some categories, especially those that may happen in the future, are much more difficult to estimate. Nonetheless, the cost is real. Here are examples of how "not developing the potential" may lead to unintended financial consequences that are easy and not easy to estimate. Poor management training may result in failing to get a contract for the following year. It might be easy to calculate the financial loss in the future — the value of the contract. When poor management training caused the failure to open a new product line, then estimating the future cost of losses might be impossible.

Similarly, the category of hidden costs such as risks may or may not have estimates of financial consequences. For example, not having adequate internet security makes an organization open to a security breach. In some industries, it is very easy to calculate the cost of a potential cyberattack. For instance, for universities, there are online calculators to estimate the cost of security breaches. If, however, an organization has a poor climate and low morale, then the risk is usually impossible to quantify financially. In the case of assessing risks from workplace accidents, it is easy to refer to past records. For example, if not shoveling snow in the entry way led to x number of accidents in the past 2 years, the annual cost of the accidents can be used when assessing future risks. However, assessing the risks hypothetically can be difficult when there are no precedents to which to refer.

In terms of precision, it may be hard to calculate the cost of a dysfunction precisely because of different actors' perception of frequency and number of dysfunctions. In these cases, the practice is to use the lowest estimate. This practice adds credibility to the hidden costs analysis, because people see that the numbers are not inflated or unreasonable.

Usually, the opposite happens — actors say that the cost of the dysfunction is higher than that estimated by the intervener-researchers.

The impact of the Mirror Effect. The mirror effect session is impactful and can be shocking. Actors may react in different ways. Some may say that this is nothing new, except they did not realize the amount of the dysfunctions and how much they cost. Some people are discouraged as they see "so much negativity," which is how they interpret the naming of what is actually happening in their organizations. Usually though, most people accept the Mirror Effect information as reasonably accurate. Overall, the biggest shock is often caused by the number of different dysfunctions and the amount of the hidden costs.

The intervener-researchers make no attempt to soften the blow, except perhaps to reassure actors that the organization is "normal," i.e., that many organizations have similar amounts of dysfunctions and hidden costs. Frequently, many actors want to start fixing dysfunctions right away and the intervener-researchers have to remind that what was presented was only symptoms of the deeper organizational problems. The organization is given a month to digest the information, to reflect on it, to live with it.

The month is the time to let the organization to unfreeze, to use Lewin's term for the process of letting go of defenses, and to become ready for organizational change. While it may look like a month of doing nothing may lead to loss of a momentum, the effect is quite opposite. Rushing the pace of change might not allow actors to fully accept the seriousness of the dysfunctions. Rushing might lead to the same old problem — fixing symptoms and not dealing with the underlying causes. A month later, the actors are introduced to a full analysis of underlying problems and possible ways to deal with them.

The Expert Opinion

A month after the Mirror Effect, the intervener-researchers deliver a second feedback session, the Expert Opinion. The term Expert Opinion reflects the nature of feedback, composed of a deeper expert analysis of organizational issues. Note that this is not "expert consulting" as described by Edgar Schein in which the consultant provides the solution to the organizational problem. The intervener-researchers use their experience

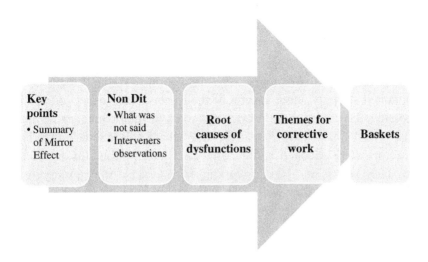

Figure. 3.5.   The process flow of the Expert Opinion feedback session.

and more than 40 years of ISEOR's research to help the organization identify the root causes of the dysfunctions.

This session is a logical movement from the problems, voiced by the actors, to bring about improvement in the projects. The goals for the intervener-researchers are (a) to remind everyone of what was said in the Mirror Effect, (b) to add the intervener-researchers' insights into what was not said, (c) to identify the root causes of the dysfunctions, (d) to offer hope to the actors in a form of corrective work, and (e) to have the actors to agree on the amount and scope of improvement work that they will undertake (Figure 3.5).

Key points. The first step of the Expert Opinion is to summarize the main points from the Mirror Effect. After the summary, the intervener-researchers ask whether they captured all the main points from the Mirror Effect correctly. If someone were to add a point, the intervener-researcher would accept this verbally, and move on.

Non Dit. "Non Dit" is French for "what was not said." The Non Dit includes the intervener-researchers' observations of what seems to be invisible, such as actors' unstated ideas and organizational taboos. This part of the presentation is, perhaps, the hardest part of the Expert Opinion to create. The intervener-researchers have to present the underlying problems in such a manner that actors can hear without feeling blamed. The intervener-researchers also need to convey the seriousness of the situation without making the actors feel hopeless.

For instance, once we worked with a group in which many actors complained strongly about several of their peers. They never raised their complaints directly to those peers, so at work the complaints came out as oblique criticisms and passive–aggressive behavior. When we pointed this out, actors were shocked to hear that such description was applied to them. They saw themselves as working hard to serve the community, as good people who meant well. The destructiveness of their behavior had never been clear to them. They challenged us and defended their behavior. We stated that each person was responsible for developing a healthy and harmonious workplace and they never talked to their peers about what behaviors have to change, but instead badmouthed the peers behind their backs. We reminded them that while the change would take some wisdom and courage, they could succeed. In the end, they could see our point and decided to work on fostering a better work climate.

Another interesting thing about the Non Dit is its method of delivery. The interveners prepare the actors that they will not see the next section of analysis on a screen, but rather they have to listen to it carefully. The interveners read each paragraph slowly, twice, which creates an introspective mood and also has a more powerful effect. The sound of intervener-researcher's voice is the only stimulus for the actors. Without any other stimuli, such as bullet points on a PowerPoint slide, actors listen more carefully. Sometimes, the effect from the Non Dit is similar to the one from a sermon in a church. After the interveners are done reading, there is still a moment of silence during which people reflect and think.

When we first learned about this process, we were skeptical and thought that Americans would not respond well to this approach. Having done the Non Dit in this audible manner many times in different organizations and with different audiences, we can confirm that it works very well.

Root causes of dysfunctions. Often, actors try to fix organizational problems, only to find that they reoccur again. If actors do not address the root causes of these problems, the solutions will not last. One of the purposes of the Expert Opinion is to identify the root causes of the dysfunctions in the organization (see Chapter 2 for the causal tree).

In the example of the actors who complained about but never spoke to some of their peers about what bothered them, the dysfunction was lack of organizational norms and rules about conflict and disagreements. There were two root causes of these dysfunctions.

One root cause was lack of steering. Managers were not directing their reports in terms of how to work with other actors. They were not giving feedback and direction to the actors. Actors were not taught the elementary conflict management tools so they would know how to respond to differences. The failure to provide this training is another example of lack of steering.

Another root cause was lack of negotiation. Because there were no healthy norms for managing conflicts, actors were afraid to address problems with many of their peers. They feared retaliation. The workplace did not feel safe, so people did not take risks. At the same time, they were frustrated, and held back when some peers needed help. Actors just needed to speak honestly to each other, and to negotiate about their needs in the workplace.

Themes for correction. After the root causes of the dysfunctions are identified, the next logical step is to outline the themes for correction. Themes imply the broader scope of general areas that need to be improved, not specific symptoms. Thus, in the example, a root cause is lack of steering, but this could be expressed more specifically, responding to the issues raised by the actors, and ideally using the words of the actors. This might be phrased as "Clarify rules of behavior and expectations for all actors."

Baskets. The final step in the flow of Expert Opinion is baskets. In France, "panniers," or bread baskets, hold a number of baguettes. In SEAM, a basket holds a number of smaller improvement projects. The intervener-researchers use the key points, Non Dit, and root causes to design baskets. The actors may accept baskets, adjust them, or add to them. While hypothetically the actors may reject baskets, practically it is hard to do so due to the transparency and logical flow of analysis. It is also possible to postpone some baskets if the time does not allow to do them all. At this point, the ownership of the basket belongs to the actors who will be the ones to design the process, actors involved, and timeline for each project that comes from a basket.

In the earlier example, the basket to address the problem might be to "develop and communicate clear goals, policies, and expectations for the organization and its actors." Actors who worked on this basket might divide it into more than one project, such as "create new strategic goals," "develop clear expectations for professional behavior for staff," and "train managers to steer."

Projects

Following the Expert Opinion, the implementation of the projects begins. The implementation phase determines whether changes in the silo or the whole organization will be sustained (see Chapter 6 for details on implementation). The intervener-researchers meet monthly with the project leaders, or with the whole project group, depending on the need and preferences of the organization. The goals of these meetings are to assist the project groups in formulating a strategy for doing the project, to encourage the group if actors become discouraged, and to help the project members develop measurement tools to determine whether the proposed changes are effectively reducing dysfunctions.

Projects should be designed to be completed in a year or less. Projects that involve actors from one silo are usually simple and can be implemented within 3 months. For projects that deal with a complex problem across different organizational silos, it is necessary to involve actors from each of the different silos. The complexity of the problem and the difficulty of matching actors' schedules influence how quickly the project can be completed. Some complex problems cannot be resolved without the involvement of the top leadership. This is why SEAM's practice of starting interventions with the top leaders makes sense. Being involved in the SEAM process themselves, the leaders are more willing to support change in individual silos, as well as be involved themselves when necessary.

Summary

The SEAM intervention is a systemic change process that involves the whole organization and consists of three simultaneous activities — the organizational improvement process, teaching managers how to use the SEAM management tools, and coaching leaders to navigate change. The intervention begins at the top and cascades down through the various organizational silos. The intervention is a rigorous and deliberately paced process, designed to identify dysfunctions and their roots, calculate hidden costs, solve problems through project groups, and train and coach managers.

Chapter 4

The SEAM Management Tools

Teaching managers the socio-economic approach to management (SEAM) management tools is one of the axes of the SEAM trihedron. Some of the SEAM management tools resemble traditional management tools. However, because the SEAM tools stem from a different mental model of management, they have a different purpose. The purpose of the SEAM management tools is to reduce dysfunctions, increase cooperation between actors, and improve steering. To help the reader to understand the socio-economic nature of the SEAM management tools, they are described in terms of their purpose, differentiation from other traditional tools, and how the tools draw on socio-economic theory. Examples of how the tools were used in organizations may create the context for a better understanding.

The Time Management Tool

The purpose of the tool. One of major problems in organizations is that many managers do not use their time effectively. There are a variety of reasons for this problem, and often the issue of using time wisely or efficiently is not addressed. The Time Management tool helps managers to analyze the use of their time throughout their work day.

Description of the tool. The tool is supposed to be filled only by managers, not by workers who report to the managers. After the managers fill in the Time Management tool, they do not have to show the findings to anyone, unless they choose to use the findings to negotiate with their bosses. For example, the tool can indicate that the manager spends much time on activities that are not important or dysfunctional. If these tasks are ordered by the manager's boss, it is important to bring this information to the boss.

There are three main sections in the tool — recording, analyzing, and making decisions. The first section requires the manager to record the tasks done during the day and the amount of time the manager spends on each task. The second section of the tool is designed to help the manager analyze the types of activities done and assess the value of each activity. The third section calls the manager to make decisions about keeping, eliminating, or delegating tasks based on the analysis of the tasks.

Recording the tasks is done throughout the work day. Analysis of the nature of the tasks can be done at the end of the day. The nature of the task can be analyzed according to five categories:

- *Routine management* — doing the usual things that managers are required to do (answering emails, providing instructions to direct reports, providing feedback to employees, meeting with people, managing conflict, etc.)
- *Regulating dysfunctions* — dealing with tasks that are dysfunctional and hurts manager's ability to work well (attending meaningless meetings, duplicating someone's work, dealing with broken equipment, etc.)
- *Shift in function* — routinely doing work that someone with lower pay might do (work of direct reports, photo copying, running errands, etc.)
- *Strategic implementation* — doing work that contributes to carrying out the department's and organization's goals (steering employees toward the strategic goals of the organization)
- *Preventing dysfunctions* — any work that is aimed at reducing dysfunctions (participating in the improvement projects, training employees, etc.)

Often, people do not know to which category a task should belong. They are afraid to be wrong in their analysis. However, because they do not have to show their Time Management tool to anyone, it is almost impossible to be wrong here. The tool is used for self-analysis and is based on actors' perceptions of the value and functionality of the task. Over time, people learn how to identify the category easily. Moreover, they learn to respect their time and choose to do dysfunctional or unimportant tasks.

What makes the tool different? Many people track their time at work in some ways or they have experienced other time assessment and Time Management tools before. The SEAM Time Management tool is different from other similar tools in its intent and analysis.

The intent of the tool is not to control and punish actors but rather to educate and help them to be effective. Behind the tool there is a belief that all actors can improve the way they work on their own. They neither need to be forced nor punished if they do not improve. Actors improve as they see the value in improving, and the revelation about the value of time occurs during the SEAM intervention. Indeed, people are motivated to improve when it makes sense to them, not because they are told so. The work of SEAM is to make the workplace climate safe and filled with hope so that actors choose to improve as soon as possible. This is why the actors do not have to show their time management exercise to others. If they had to show the exercise findings to their managers, there would be the risk of false reporting, so that actors would look good in their manager's eyes.

The analysis section of the tool allows managers to identify how much time is spent on dysfunctions, how much time is spent on steering and strategic work, and how often they are interrupted. Usually, the time assessment exercise makes managers realize that they spend far too little time steering, leading and managing actors, in order to create a cohesive workplace. In fact, they may realize that 30–50% of their time is doing dysfunctional work, such as duplicating tasks, covering for direct reports, attending useless meetings, and so on. This realization helps managers make decisions about which tasks they want to keep, which tasks will be eliminated, or delegated. Of course, it may take some time for managers to accept the necessity of change and they may need some confidence to do that, but once they start changing, they become much more effective managers.

Link to socio-economic theory. Socio-economic theory shapes the use of the Time Management tool. The primary root cause of dysfunctions is lack of steering. Managers' main task is to steer their part of the organization, aligning people and resources to accomplish the strategic goals of the organization. If a manager does not spend enough time steering, the result will be poorer performance of the manager's department or unit. In a way, the Time Management tool is a mirror that shows managers if they are spending enough time steering, or if they are letting other tasks divert them from the essential and core managerial job. We have found that managers rarely assess how much time they spend steering. Yet, without steering, it is hard to expect the organization or any of its parts to be effective.

Another root cause of dysfunctions is the lack of cleaning up. Each time someone adds something to the list of things to do, something else must be reduced or deleted, or delegated. The Time Management tool helps identify the dysfunctions that come from trying to add more and more to one's plate, without taking a serious look at the magical thinking that is rampant in modern organization. See more about magical thinking in Chapter 5. Actors pretend they can keep doing more and more tasks without either burning out or performing poorly.

Example. Here are two examples of the use of the Time Management tool. One factor that can lead to fairly large hidden costs is attending useless and poorly led management meetings. While numerous and useless meetings are a frequent complaint in the workplace, without quantifying how much time is wasted, the waste tends to be ignored. If a manager finds that time is wasted in meetings, correcting the problem can save time for everybody.

In one middle-sized organization, the senior leader group meetings were always led by the CEO. At those meetings, the leaders frequently strayed off task, often did not reach decisions, and if they did make a decision, later they could not agree what the decision was. All of the six executives on the leadership group listed these meetings as wasted time. They met for 3 hours per week, and at least half of the time was not productive. Over a year this added up to 432 hours of time that could have been used much more efficiently. The value of the time was over $30,000. After seeing the assessment of wasted time, the group members decided to take turns in being facilitators, to prepare meeting agendas ahead of time, and to record what decisions were made and when to revisit those decisions. Their meetings became much more effective, which had a positive impact on their morale and their ability to steer the organization.

Another factor that can lead to very large hidden costs is having a great number of interruptions. When one is involved in a task and is interrupted, after the interruption it takes time to refocus on the original task. If the task is simple, it may take 30 seconds, but if the task is complex, or requires re-opening numerous computer programs, then starting again can take much more time. The time to get back on task is rework, wasted time.

In a department of 30 people, the supervisors saw that their own time wasted due to interruptions was also a problem with all actors. While they realized the size of the dysfunction, their willingness to reduce the time spent on interruptions did not change until it became personal — through their Time Management tool. The value of the hidden cost of interruptions was $324,000. By reorganizing the work, the actors were able to cut in half the wasted time due to interruptions.

The Competency Grid

The purpose of the tool. In order to work effectively, a department must have actors with the skills needed to do the work. That sounds obvious, but too often managers have not made a systematic assessment of actors' competencies needed for the department's successful work currently and in the future. Most managers assess intuitively, which leads to several problems. One problem is that, without mapping competencies in a systematic analysis, it is possible to be inaccurate or even miss the skills that the department needs. Second, intuitive assessments may overlook what skills will be needed in the future for developments in the department. Third, without having a systemic view of all actors' skills, it is hard to identify training needs. The competency grid helps managers and actors to choose together the best training — training that helps the department succeed and that grows actors' human potential.

Description of the tool. The Competency Grid is a simple table with two axes. On one axis of the grid, there is a list of all skills needed for a department to operate efficiently. The other axis lists all actors in the department. There are two steps in working with this tool — creating the Competency Grid and filling it in.

Creating the grid ought to be a department project, made collectively, so that all requisite skills are present and all actors in the department believe the grid is accurate. This collective exercise helps everyone in the department to see the skills that are needed to work in the present, in the future, and skills needed to advance into a supervisory position.

Filling in the grid is done individually by each actor and supervisor. They fill in their perception of the actor's skill levels. The markings of the grid indicate whether an actor has mastered the skill, has the skill but is not yet proficient, knows the principles but has not used the skill, or has no ability or knowledge of the skill. Completing the Competency Grid needs to be kept separate from discussion about wages or raise. Instead, the Competency Grid can be the beginning of a discussion between manager and employee about the employee's level of development and what the employee might want to learn. The goal of the discussion is first to identify the interests of the actor and the needs of the department and then to agree on future development for the actor.

When the grid is completed, the areas of strength and weakness for current and future work are easily observable. The Competency Grid serves as a map that guides a manager's decisions about hiring actors who have the needed skills, developing skills internally, cross-training, and what tasks might need to be outsourced. Seeing the areas of missing skills can also help a manager plan for what to do when someone with an important skill is absent due to vacation, illness, or emergency, or leaving the department (see Figure 4.1).

Some actors may be anxious about having a Competency Grid in which all actors are named, so their abilities can be seen and discussed publicly. The grid is most useful when all actors in the department can see the results for each person. All actors have different skills and knowing who can do what allows for teams to be more self-managing. However, if a department is not ready for such self-disclosure, the manager can substitute a number for each name, so all can see the skill level of the department without any risk of embarrassment.

The Competency Grid shown in Figure 4.1 is a little different from the ISEOR model. ISEOR lists skills for operations (day-to-day and

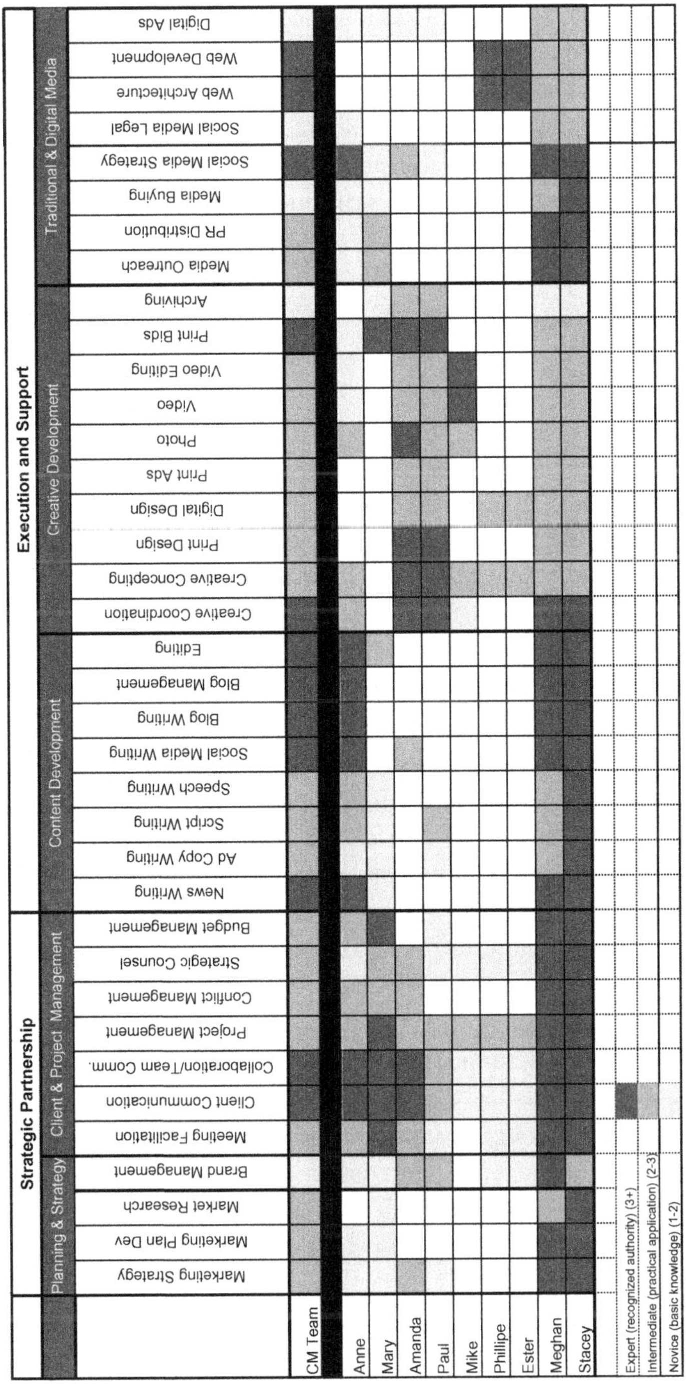

Figure 4.1. The Competency Grid maps the actors' skills available in the department.

development work), specific know-how, and new operations to be developed. Our list included skills for current operations, interpersonal skills, supervisory skills, and skills for future development. We have found that often managers do not think through the interpersonal skills needed in the department, such as the ability to listen well, or manage conflicts, or calm angry customers. Identifying which skills are needed, as well as assessing the ability of each actor, is the first step in the development of creating a training program. Additionally, listing the supervisory skills achieves three goals. First, it helps a supervisor to identify personal areas of weakness that need development. Second, having supervisory skills listed allows those employees who want to become supervisors at some point, prepare themselves for that move in their careers. Third, when hiring supervisors, the grid identifies the competencies that are needed in the person being hired.

What makes the tool different? As with any other SEAM management tools, the Competency Grid does not have a punitive feel. The purpose of the tool is not to judge actors but to help them identify their areas of development. This tool is very instrumental in developing actors' human potential, which needs to be done in a collaborative manner.

The tool fosters the participation of and cohesion among actors. Creating the Competency Grid and thinking through all the skills needed for the department to succeed is a collective exercise. This exercise includes the actors' input and thus allows them to be part of important decisions about hiring or training. The manager and all actors together see the extent to which the needed skills are present and lacking. All actors become engaged and interested in making sure their departments have all competencies needed to work well.

There is a difference between the Competency Grid and a job description. Usually, human resource job descriptions do not list all skills in such a comprehensive way as the Competency Grid. The Competency Grid is made by the people doing the actual work. The Competency Grid can inform the human resources department, or can be a separate list to use in the hiring process. Many managers, after working with the Competency Grid, have commented that they wish they had learned about this tool before a recent hiring process.

An ever-present task at all levels of an organization is how to develop succession planning. Are there actors who have the skills to move up the hierarchical ladder when there is an opening or the desire to learn supervisory skills? In developing leadership from within the organization, preparing actors for increased managerial and leadership responsibilities is necessary. Thus, including the supervisory skills on the Competency Grid makes the skills needed obvious to all actors. Actors who want to move up the hierarchical ladder have a roadmap for competencies needed for advancement.

Link to socio-economic theory. At the heart of the socio-economic theory is the belief that developing the potential of all actors in an organization is the only way to create significant and sustainable change that adds value to the organization. The question then becomes how to help each actor develop. Actors' interests and aptitudes have to be meshed with the organization's needs for productivity. The Competency Grid is a tool that allows for a systematic assessment of the current and future status of skills. It is developed with the participation all actors, which increases the accuracy of the tool.

One of the root causes of organizational dysfunctions is the lack of negotiation. Developing human potential requires negotiation. Managers and employees need to talk about the employee's level of skill, and where the employee wants to grow. The Competency Grid assists the negotiation in two ways. First, the development of the Competency Grid requires managers and employees to negotiate about the levels of the employee's skills. Although a manager or employee might fear negotiations about an employee's level of competency, such dialogue is necessary. Negotiation is the way to have accurate data, remove false impressions, and establish trust among all actors.

Second, the negotiation helps actors think about developing their human potential. Some actors have career plans and some actors do not. The negotiation with the supervisor allows actors to think about how they want to grow and negotiate the development plan.

Example. In one technological department, supervisors were usually technicians who were promoted and did not receive any training for the new position. The technicians saw supervision as another add-on task, for which they were not rewarded. As result, there was conflict in the department, tension between supervisors and employees, and low morale. When a Competency Grid was made for the supervisors, the actors began to understand what skills and competencies were needed to be a good supervisor. The group of new supervisors helped shape their own supervisory training and collectively developed a consistent approach to supervision throughout the department. Over the course of a year, they gained confidence and greatly improved their supervisory skills.

Internal/External Strategic Action Plan

The purpose of the tool. The Internal/External Strategic Action Plan helps the organization to set the long-term strategic goals and develop objectives and actions to achieve these goals.

Description of the tool. The Internal/External Strategic Plan has two sets of goals — internal and external. The internal goals include any activities to reduce dysfunctions, make the organization more effective, and support external efforts. External goals focus on strategic development: growth, increasing market share and profits, and developing new products. Having both categories is essential.

Socio-economic theory postulates that when an organization reduces dysfunctions and hidden costs, the organization may invest released resources in the external goals. In other words, the Internal plan helps fund the External plan, and the organization self-finances its development through reduction of hidden costs.

The Internal/External Strategic Action Plan tool is a simple table in which the leaders identify the strategic goals of the organization and the actors responsible for achieving each goal. Goals are broken into objectives and actions steps. The steps are then plotted in 6-month periods for 3 years. Identifying steps and a timeline is standard in good strategic planning.

What makes the tool different? The incorporation of internal and external goals makes the Internal/External Strategic Action Plan different from traditional strategic plans. The internal goals focus on reducing dysfunctions and hidden costs that can be barriers to achieving the external goals.

Table 4.1. Internal/External strategic action plan.

Strategic goals	Priority objectives	Priority actions	People in charge	Year 1 in 6-month periods		Year 2 in 6-month periods		Year 3 in 6-month periods	
				1	2	1	2	1	2
Internal strategic goals 1. 2. 3.									
External strategic goals 1. 2. 3.									

Another difference is that traditional strategic plans, while spelling out strategic goals and timeline, may be detached from the activities of the lower organizational levels. The unique feature of the Internal/External Strategic Action Plan is that it serves as a basis for actors' goals and priorities. Each manager's Priority Action Plan begins with the Internal/External Strategic Action Plan, so actions to achieve the goals cascade strategic priorities down throughout the organization.

Link to socio-economic theory. The Internal/External Strategic Action Plan gives management and employees a clear idea of what is important in the next 3–5 years for the development of their organization, and their role in this plan. This is in sync with the socio-economic theory, in which all actors are important in fulfilling organizational goals. If all actors know how their efforts fit together and what is their role in achieving strategic goals, then it is more likely that actors will be engaged and committed to implementing strategic plans.

Example. In a transportation company, a group of mechanics routinely fixed busses and equipment without being much aware of what else was happening in the organization. Because they fixed problems, the mechanics knew which drivers needed more repairs on their busses. The mechanics never shared this information, as they thought nobody would listen to them. After seeing the new Internal/External Strategic Action Plan of the organization, they recognized their role in the most important organizational priority of customer safety. As a result, the group became the information hub feeding information to the training department about training needs. After the trainers refocused their work based on the mechanics input, the accident and repair rate declined by 20%.

The end of the story is even more inspiring. The mechanics realized that on one type of bus there was a flaw in the design of the engine. The chief mechanic went to the headquarters of the bus company to explain how they could improve the engines, which the bus company did. Before SEAM, the mechanics expected no one would listen to them. After SEAM, the mechanics became proactive and saw their insights turn into improved engine design and customer safety.

How did the Internal/External Strategic Action Plan make a difference? When the mechanics saw the priorities spelled out and talked about their role in fulfilling the priorities, they realized how their work fit into the larger plan.

The Priority Action Plan

Implementing a strategic plan calls for the coordinated actions by many people. At the same time, managers have to continue to do their regular managerial tasks. Keeping a balance between ongoing work and new developments can be a challenge, especially in the context of coordination with many other actors.

The purpose of the tool. The Priority Action Plan helps managers to identify tasks that have a high value for achieving the strategic goals of the organization. The Priority Action Plan also outlines tasks that have a low value in achieving organizational strategic objectives and eliminates such tasks. Identifying the low-value tasks that eat up time from achieving strategic goals becomes part of the negotiation with the actor's supervisor about which tasks should be kept, delegated, or eliminated.

Description of the tool. The CEO creates the first Priority Action Plan based on the priorities identified in the Internal/External Strategic

Action Plan. Using the CEO's plan, the next layer of managers draw up their plans, and share them with the CEO and each other. At this point, the top-level leadership is aware of the organizational strategic goals and of its own strategic priorities. Work throughout the organization is increasingly aligned. Then the next layer of managers take their supervisor's Priority Action Plans and draw up their own. This process of cascading priorities down through the organization continues until the priorities of all managers at all organizational levels are identified and aligned.

The Priority Action Plan is a grid with columns for strategic goals, priority objectives, priority actions, departments or people involved, forecast planning, and comments. The first column of the Priority Action Plan begins with the goals from the Internal/External Strategic Action Plan in which the actor has a part.

The "priority objectives" are the specific results agreed upon to achieve the goals. The "priority actions" are the concrete acts to take place in the next 6 months. "People involved" is a list of people from different departments, who are responsible for the actions. "Forecast planning" breaks the 6-month period into monthly segments; this makes it is easy to see when and what tasks will be done.

ISEOR posits four aspects of the Priority Action Plan:

1. Spurring — Pushing the implementation of the Internal/External Strategic Action Plan through translating strategic objectives into priority objectives, and then into priority actions for each actor involved.
2. Decentralizing — Getting commitment from the actors involved in various tasks. The outcomes of decentralization are clarity about tasks assigned to each actor, and elimination of duplication. The plan also lays the groundwork for delegation of tasks by pushing decision-making as low as possible in the organization.
3. Synchronizing — Coordinating all efforts through scheduling priorities for the actors involved.
4. Enhancing vigilance — Avoiding or overcoming possible barriers to successful implementation. The last column of the tool includes actors' comments about the barriers that might disrupt the work and remind the owner of the Priority Action Plan to prepare for overcoming resistance.

Table 4.2. A sample of priority action plan.

Strategic goals	Priority objectives	Priority actions	People involved	Forecast planning hours of work needed in next 6 months						Comments
				1	2	3	4	5	6	
Goal 1										
Goal 2										
....										
Regular work										
Emergencies										
Vacations										
Total hours										

The example of the Priority Action Plan presented above is a little different from the tool used by ISEOR. In response to the chronic inability of many managers to manage their time well, we added to the tool two new elements. One addition is an estimated number of hours needed per month to complete each Priority Action. Another element is incorporation of three other categories of work into the plan that managers usually do — routine work, emergencies, and vacations or time off. Planning the time for these categories of work makes actors much more aware of how much time will be spent on strategic objectives. The bottom row of Table 4.2 contains the total amount of hours needed per completion of each priority.

Completing the Priority Action Plan helps an actor see whether the amount of time to do all priorities is reasonable. When an actor sees that there is not enough time in the day to complete all the priorities, the actor needs to negotiate with his or her supervisor about what the actor's priorities should be. The goal of the tool is to help actors learn to prioritize their tasks, and to prepare them for negotiation about time and priorities.

What makes the tool different? The Priority Action Plan provides means to synchronize organizational efforts and enhance teamwork.

Because individual Priority Action Plans stem from actors' and supervisors' Priority Action Plans, and the organizational strategic goals, there is a synergetic effect across organizational silos. This synergy allows to align resources and efforts rather than dispersing them.

Another difference is that the Priority Action Plan provides actors with data to negotiate with their managers when expectations of work become unrealistic. The negotiation between actor and actor's supervisor is essential. Supervisors learn about the time needed to do the tasks under their realm of responsibility and help the actors to shape the priorities, so that all actions are aligned toward the organization's goals. Actors feel the respect that comes from having their needs accepted, rather than being told to do more than is possible. Part of the negotiation is agreeing on what the actors will not do.

Link to socio-economic theory. Lack of synchronization is one of the root causes of hidden costs. The Priority Action Plan focuses on synchronizing the efforts and activities of all actors. It also takes into account the time and other resources that are needed by the actor to complete important tasks.

The Priority Action Plan is a good example of the shift from the top-down management style to the participative approach of socio-economic theory. Rather than order an actor what to do, reason comes into play and the actor can negotiate priorities. The trust and respect of an actor that allow for such negotiation is a hallmark of socio-economic theory.

Example. One top executive was working over 80 or 90 hours per week. She was willing to do this for a brief period to help the organization. Yet, working for many months in this pace, without any change in sight, took toll on her. She felt exhausted, began to develop health issues, and was losing interest in work. She was burning out. Part of the problem was that she was very loyal to the organization, so she pushed herself to overwork. Part of the problem was lack of resources to take over her specific duties. After completing the Priority Action Plan, she had data to negotiate her priorities with the CEO. Some things were removed from her priorities, and some were delayed. Seeing the unreasonable number of hours in the tool led her to give herself permission to work less. Later, reflecting on the situation, she was aware that the tool helped her to see the insanity of how much time she devoted to work. She was pleased that, through negotiation, she reorganized her work priorities and made more time for her family.

The Strategic Piloting Logbook

Managers have many different tasks and activities. It can be difficult to keep all information at one's fingertips. As SEAM develops in the organization, and new activities are designed, managers need to keep track of more information. It is easy to lose things if one is not organized. Searching for documents can quickly become a time-wasting dysfunction. This is where the Strategic Piloting Logbook becomes useful.

The purpose of the tool. The Strategic Piloting Logbook is the series of indicators that are created to keep the organization on course, which is directed at its strategic goals. The Piloting Logbook has two functions. One is to be a reminder of all of the decisions and events in the SEAM intervention. The other is to bring together different sources of information to assist in assessment of progress and to aid in decision-making.

A Piloting Logbook should allow a manager to find, quickly and easily, the following information:

- Indicators needed for making decisions in one's area of responsibility.
- Indicators needed for reporting to one's hierarchical superior. Indicators are measurements of significant and relevant information. Indicators can be qualitative, quantitative, and financial.
- Information that should be regularly transmitted to one's subordinates.
- Data that are necessary for responding to exterior partners' questions (e.g., governmental regulations).
- The Internal/External Strategic Action Plan and the Priority Action Plan of one's manager, oneself, and one's direct reports.
- Minutes from projects.

What makes the tool different? The Strategic Piloting Logbook is a commonsense way to keep information organized. What is different is that most managers throughout the organization do not have a common place where all decisions about their strategic priorities and indicators of work being done are readily accessible.

When SEAM has been implemented, managers using the Logbook have instant access to the planning documents for the organization, including documents of their managers, direct reports, and their own. Managers also have access to the measures that come from projects. The tool reinforces intra-organizational communication, as every manager has information about goals and decisions across different projects and priorities. This information, in turn, enhances synchronization and cooperation of all actors and silos.

Link to socio-economic theory. Steering involves knowing the goals of the organization, knowing how specifically each goal will be implemented, knowing who will be involved and when, and reviewing incoming data to make sure that the organization is on track to meet its goals. When managers lose track of some of the data, they cannot steer well. The intent is alignment of all the parts of the organization, so "the ship stays on course."

Example. At ISEOR, all actors have their Logbooks, which are paper notebooks. Information about the decisions made at a meeting from several months ago can be retrieved quickly. In the United States, most managers who underwent a SEAM intervention have opted for an electronic Logbook. Documents such as Priority Action Plans tend to be shared electronically, and are filed and shared electronically on a common platform. In a meeting, it is easy to quickly access the Logbook information, share it on a screen, or send any part of the information to anyone, electronically.

Periodically Negotiated Activity Contract

One of the purposes of SEAM is to help organizations become more productive. In for-profit organizations, this effort results in more profit. When actors work hard to grow profits, and the gain is taken by top managers and shareholders, the risk of resentment and disengagement is high.

In the non-profit world, everything from government to hospitals to education to the multitude of service organizations, actors are expected to help achieve the organizational mission rather than return a profit. If actors succeed in delivering more services in a cost-effective manner, they also deserve to be rewarded some of the gain. When the gain is not shared, this may also lead to resentment.

The purpose of the tool. The Periodically Negotiated Activity Contract allows the organization and its employees to negotiate the efforts required for successful implementation of Priority Action Plan, and the potential rewards to the actor.

The Periodically Negotiated Activity Contract is created for 6 months through dialogue with one's immediate supervisor. What is negotiated are expectations for improvement and how to measure these. Actors and their supervisors have to agree upon which improvements will be rewarded and how the improvements will be assessed. However, the actual amount of the bonus for improved performance is not negotiated — it is a fixed rate for the whole organization.

What makes the tool different? There are different ways to reward employees for helping an organization succeed. Profit sharing is practiced in many organizations. What might be different is that the negotiating profit sharing is built into the organization's routine. Negotiating the contract between employee and manager reinforces the respect for every actor.

Link to socio-economic theory. One goal of SEAM is to develop human potential so that organizations can be more productive. When SEAM improves the economic effectiveness of an organization, then the question arises: who should get the increased profit? In the socio-economic theory, some of the profits should go to reward the actors who contributed in the improvement.

The Periodically Negotiated Activity Contract draws on several socio-economic themes. It is respectful of the organization and each individual. It is highly participative in nature. It rewards the development of the actor's potential.

Example. Jean Caghasi is a French business director who led the takeover of a French company and wrote about his SEAM experience. He described his purpose for seeking out SEAM:

> Just before the take-over, I was planning to implement a pay-rewarding system based on objectives. I had heard about ISEOR and discovered the SEAM method. In fact, it was more than what I had initially envisioned — SEAM was a fully integrated management system.... I can confirm that

the performance pay-rewarding system is the cornerstone of the SEAM management practice. It took 2 years to build up a battery of performance indicators, which are essential for feedback in the system. Those indicators had to be objective, and not dependent on anything else than a measure of guaranteed performance. (2004, pp. 108–109)

The Delegation Tool

Many managers do not spend enough time for steering. Their time is dissipated by other activities. One of the ways for them to increase time for steering is to delegate some of their current work to other actors. One of the excuses that managers use in explaining their inability to delegate is not having people with the skills needed to do the work at a sufficient level of quality. Managers are sometimes afraid that training and monitoring people will take much of their time and so it is quicker to do the work themselves. Other excuses on the part of managers are that they have not thought through what can be delegated, or they are so busy that taking on another task of delegating is beyond their time and energy level.

The purpose of the tool. The Delegation tool is designed (a) to allow managers to assess all the tasks that they might delegate, and (b) to provide a template for the negotiation with the actor to whom the tasks might be delegated. Overall, the goals of delegation are to free up the manager's time, to increase the quality of decision-making, and to develop the potential of actors by giving them new opportunities.

Description of the tool. The concept of the Delegation tool is quite simple. The issue in any delegation is decision-making. How does a manager give someone else the authority to make a decision, without losing control over the quality of the work?

There are four levels of authority in decision-making:

1. Decisions are made by the manager after consultation with the actor.
2. Decisions are made by the actor after consultation with the manager.
3. Decisions are made by the actor, who then informs the manager about the issues and the decision made.
4. Decisions are made by the actor without informing the manager about the issues and the decision made.

Table 4.3. A sample of the Delegation tool.

Decisions	Levels of authority decisions are made by			
	1. Manager, after consulting with actor	2. Actor, after consulting with manager	3. Actor, informing manager later	4. Actor, without informing manager

When a manager meets with an actor, a list of possible decisions that are made concerning the actor's area of responsibility is composed. A grid can be created. One axis lists all the decisions to be made. On the other axis are the four levels of authority of decision-making. The first goal is to assess the mutual understanding of what is expected about decision-making. The second task is to explore how to move decisions from column 1 to column 4 (Table 4.3). Each movement toward increasing the actor's authority to make decisions means less time spent by the manager on the task and more time is freed for steering.

What makes the tool different? The Delegation tool is another example of common sense at work. However, usually, managers do not assess the decisions they can delegate in a systematic manner. Thus, this tool helps a manager to look at all the decisions to be made in the unit and delegate some of the decisions to actors. Another difference is that decisions delegated are in writing and negotiated. In this way, both a manager and actor create the same expectations and address any concerns. After the expectations are set and concerns are addressed, the Delegation tool serves as an indicator of established authority over certain decisions, setting the completion of the tool.

Link to socio-economic theory. In socio-economic theory, lack of steering is the greatest of the root causes of dysfunctions. The Delegation tool allows managers to free up time for steering. Additionally, the cornerstone principle of socio-economic theory is apparent in this tool: increasing effectiveness by developing human potential. By increasing actors' authority over some decisions, the Delegation tool helps actors develop their decision-making skills.

Example. In one organization, executives were overwhelmed with tasks and often talked about the need to delegate. However, nothing changed. Executives kept doing a lot of operational work, which their employees perceived as micromanagement. One executive took the Delegation tool to heart and decided to apply it in her work with one of the new mid-level managers in the organization.

The new manager was a very detail-oriented person and the meetings of the executive and this manager had been filled with discussion of operational issues. There was no time left to plan and discuss high-level issues and projects. The executive decided to try the Delegation tool. They both discussed the level of required decision-making and the expectations regarding communication. The executive freed up some of her time. The Delegation tool proved to be effective in building the confidence level of the new manager and ensuring that decisions were made at the right level by the right people. The new manager also learned to utilize this tool with her managers and team members, giving them more authority and allowing them to perform to their potential.

Summary

The SEAM management tools provide a simple and effective way for managers to set priorities, manage their time, coordinate work of other actors and departments, and making sure that actors and departments have the right competencies to do work.

The tools reinforce each other and collectively they create a managerial structure that helps the organization increase its effectiveness. For instance, when managers become aware of their use of time with the Time Management tool, they can identify important tasks that go into the Priority Action Plan. The Internal/External Strategic Action Plan spells out developments for the future, which informs the need to develop future skills, and thus they are listed in the Competency Grid. Implicit in the all tools are the socio-economic tenets of respect for every actor, and creating a healthy management system. Every manager learns how to manage well and steer actors toward strategic goals.

Chapter 5

The Theoretical Roots
of SEAM

The socio-economic theory is built on many different disciplines, and at least two major disciplines influenced the thinking of Henri Savall. First, Savall drew on economists of 20th century, especially Germán Bernácer, the Spanish economist and physicist, and the French economist François Perroux. He also discovered the field of European and Northern American Organization Development (OD) and was influenced by some authors and schools of thought. This chapter provides a very brief summary of the theories of scholars that provided the context for the socio-economic theory.

Economic Influences on SEAM

Germán Bernácer (1883–1965). Bernácer, trained in physics and self-taught in economics, was the subject of Savall's first doctoral thesis. In his first book in 1916, *Happiness and Society: Essay on Social Mechanics*, Bernácer wrote about concepts that would later be described as Keynesian, but he was never completely in agreement with Keynes. Keynes published his *General Theory of Employment, Interest and Money in 1936*. Bernácer was one of the earliest critics, pointing out the gaps in the theory.

Core to the value system of Bernácer was the belief that every person has a status as an individual who has a certain amount of autonomy, and, at the same time, status as a member of society. In other words, people are free to make their own choices within limits, which are determined by their own inner awareness and external laws. People as members of society are nurtured by society, and in return, they owe to society care for the common good.

In Keynesian economics, a certain amount of unemployment is thought to be unavoidable. The role of the state is to guard for monetary stability by adjusting the interest rate. Bernácer concluded that unemployment is a fallacy of Keynesian thought. Savall (2017) summed up Bernácer's argument:

> Bernácer argued against the high level of employment which came with Keynesian economics by introducing an ethical condition. Each human being lives only thanks to the labor supplied by the community, which results from the total of each individual's work. This labor is applied to the physical world (land, natural resources in general) and to the intangible (natural human skills) in order to provide products. The only activity that legitimates the ownership of the product is human labor in all its forms: manual work, administrative work, supervision, management, and coordination. Each form of necessary work is useful to produce goods and services in order to satisfy human needs. The division of work implies solidarity among those who work, and thus the abolition of any individual income that is not engendered by one's current or former labor. Consequently, the political and social organization has to allow all persons to assume their productive role for society, without any form of restriction. Unemployment is, in a way, the entropy of the system. Unemployment is not inevitable. It is just the natural deterioration process of energy due to time, and this can be overcome. (p. 11)

One of Bernácer's radical assertions was that unearned income, and materials that were subject to speculation, were harmful to society and should be abolished. One can see the thought of Bernácer in the socio-economic theory. SEAM starts with the premise that every person has potential, and using this potential is part of leading a good life. Because every person has potential, the task of the organization, which is done by managers, is to tap this potential for the enrichment of the person and of the organization. Thus, when an organization has an economic crisis, the response is not to fire people. The response should be to grow the organization by using the untapped human potential.

One argument against quickly firing people in times of economic crisis is that, in the long run, the organization loses more money by firing employees. When the economic downturn is over, the organization has to hire and train new workers, and the cost frequently exceeds the savings from firing people. Socio-economic theory recognizes the fact that keeping employees during crisis saves the organization money in the long run. Additionally, the growth of an organization is the result of human potential, so potential must be nurtured.

According to Bernácer, every organization has an ethical obligation to protect the employee from unemployment if possible. Employment is an unspoken social contract. People live to fulfill themselves and to give to society through their work. Organizations exist to provide goods to society, wealth to owners, and employment to workers.

François Perroux (1903–1987). François Perroux was a French economist and his thoughts were parallel to those of Bernácer. François Perroux rejected the ideas of two dominant schools of economics, the neo-classical and the Marxist, and instead integrated some aspects of each school. He also rejected the claim of economists to be able to remain neutral, i.e., unbiased, in their scientific work. Perroux argued that researchers or scientists analyze data through their own sense of what is real, which means that perfect neutrality is impossible. This insight is implicitly an argument against the ability of economists or social scientists to be perfectly objective, which challenged the belief that research about management can be "scientific" in the sense of positivistic science.

For Perroux, creativity is essentially collective. An individual can create, to be sure, but the act of creation is always in a context of ideas shared by others. The implication is that improving an organization must be based on improving the collective situation, not on developing individualistic stars. In other words, the key to creativity is the system, not merely the bright individual.

Perroux wrote about imbalances that weakened economic performance, and Savall equated these imbalances to dysfunctions. For Savall,

> The SEAM intervention aims at mastering the imbalances, not annihilating them but transforming them. The goal is to arrive at effective and efficient balances which are socially sustainably. The method is fostering social dialog which allows social groups to make projects and plans and thus to make possible the additive allocation of resources necessary to the realization of those plans. (Savall, 2017, p. 17)

OD Influences on SEAM

Kurt Lewin (1890–1947). Kurt Lewin, a German-American psychologist, was educated in Germany and came to the US before World War II. He studied group dynamics, force field analysis, conflict, and organizational change and is considered the founder of social psychology.

According to Lewin, groups will be more likely to change and adopt new ideas if they are part of creating the ideas. Groups tend to resist change, so the starting point is helping the group let go of defensiveness and become open to the possibility of change. The change process that Lewin described was "unfreezing, changing, freezing" and Lewin used action research to unfreeze a group. His action research seems simple. The consultant works with a group by listening to the group's concerns and synthesizing what the group said. Then the consultant provides feedback to the group, which affirms or corrects the content of concerns. Finally, the consultant works with the group to improve the situation. What is radical in action research is the premise that the group has the knowledge to make changes. This is the opposite of the common belief that leaders are the only ones with the ability to correct problems within the workplace.

In SEAM, the unfreezing process takes 2 months. After interviews, the group waits a month before receiving the Mirror Effect. In addition to the typical action research feedback, dysfunctions are categorized and hidden costs are calculated. A month later, the Expert Opinion introduces the voice of the intervener-researchers in the "Non Dit" part (see the

SEAM intervention process). At this point, most participants have unfrozen and have accepted the fact of the existing dysfunctions and the need to change. People now are ready to start improvement projects to reduce dysfunctions and hidden costs.

Maslow and Hertzberg. OD was influenced by the development of humanistic psychology, which was championed by Abraham Maslow (1908–1970). Maslow, a psychologist, is well known for his hierarchy of human needs, in which the assumption is that every person can grow through stages to reach self-actualization.

Underlying the Maslow hierarchy is the positive belief that every human being has potential. Self-actualization is the fulfillment of the human being's potential. Movement through the needs to self-actualization can be blocked, for instance, by the lack of freedom of speech. The point is that the potential for growth is in all persons, not a select few. This belief in human potential is contradictory to the Taylorism, Fayolism, Weberism (TFW) virus belief that leaders are somehow more special and more deserving than the rest of humanity.

Frederick Hertzberg (1923–2000) was a psychologist who studied sources of motivation in the workplace. He claimed that the frequently used belief about motivation to "kick the person in the pants" was not really effective. We would add here that the "kick in the pants" approach

Figure 5.1.   Maslow's hierarchy of needs.

is a belief that is part of the TFW virus. His famous two-factor theory posits that there are two kinds of influences on motivation. Hygiene factors include "company policy and administration, supervision, interpersonal relationships, working conditions, salary, status, and security" (Hertzberg, 1987, p. 113). These factors do not actually motivate workers, but their absence lowers motivation. Motivational factors include "achievement, recognition for achievement, the work itself, responsibility, and growth or advancement". The presence of motivational factors increases workers' motivation.

In their time, Maslow and Hertzberg challenged the current beliefs about people and the workplace. Their recognition of the need to attend to the "socio" side of the workplace laid the groundwork for the human side of socio-economic theory.

Rensis Likert (1903–1981). Rensis Likert was an American social psychologist, known for developing the research practice of open-ended interviewing, and inventing the Likert scale, a psychometric scale for measuring people's attitudes. His work on management styles is reflected in the SEAM approach to management. In *The Human Organization: Its Management and Value* (1967), Likert described four approaches to management:

System 1: Exploitative authoritative. Managers use threats and punishments to motivate workers. Decisions are made at the top, and often managers are unaware of the problems faced by workers. Workers tend to be hostile to the organization.

System 2: Benevolent authoritative. Motivation comes through a mix of threat and reward. Major decisions are made at the top, but workers can have some say in minor decisions. Workers' satisfaction tends to be low, and productivity is better than in the exploitative authoritative system.

System 3: Consultative. Motivation is developed through rewards and occasional punishments. Major decisions are made at the top, but managers do listen to workers. Workers' satisfaction and productivity are higher than in the benevolent authoritative system.

System 4: Participative. Motivation is the result of monetary rewards and participation in goal setting. Communication flows freely, workers are fully involved in decision-making and goal setting. Workers' satisfaction and productivity are higher than in the consultative system. Table 5.1 provides a snapshot of comparison of management styles.

One of the goals in any organization is reducing costs. Likert wrote that "the usual cost reduction efforts with a shift toward System 1 are generally initiated by decisions at the top of the organization" (p. 84) and take place over several years by reducing staff, budgets, research, and development. "Standards are introduced or extended to more jobs and tightened, and increased pressure is applied to get performance to standard" (pp. 84–85). In the short run, there is a rapid rise of productivity and cost reduction. However, after 6–12 months, there is a rise in employee turnover and absences, strikes, and a reduction in quality or products and services and customer loyalty, so that by the end of 4 years, the gains in productivity and cost reduction are lost.

When an organization uses participative management, the gains in productivity and cost reduction are slower to start, taking about a year. After 2 years, turnover and absences are reduced, labor relations are improved, and product and service quality are raised. After 3 years, the gains are greater than that under System 1. Through participative management, the gains in production and cost reduction are sustainable.

Another feature of participative management is that management's knowledge grows and keeps growing. Under System 1, there is a quick spike in knowledge growth and then a sharp drop off. Likert (1967) concluded,

The highest productivity, best performance, and highest earnings appear at present to be achieved by System 4 organizations. These organizations mobilize both the noneconomic motives and economic needs so that all available motivational forces create cooperative behavior focused on achieving the organization's objectives. The enterprise is a tightly knit, well-coordinated organization of highly motivated persons. (p. 106)

Table 5.1.   Comparison of management styles.

Management style	Exploitative authoritative	Benevolent authoritative	Consultative	Participative
Responsibility	Lies in the hands of the people at the top	Lies at the managerial levels	Is spread widely through the organizational hierarchy	Is widespread throughout the organization
Trust and confidence	Superior has no trust and confidence in subordinates	Superior has condescending confidence in subordinates (master–servant relationship)	Superior has substantial but not complete confidence in subordinates	Superior has a high level of confidence in subordinates
How decisions are made	Imposed on subordinates, who do not feel free to discuss things about the job, with their superior	Subordinates do not feel free to discuss things about the job, with their superior	Some amount of discussion about job-related things, between the superior and subordinates	High level of participation
Teamwork	Little teamwork or communication	Little teamwork or communication	A fair amount of teamwork	High level of teamwork, communication, and participation
Motivation	Motivation is based on threats	Motivation is based on a system of rewards	Motivation is based on rewards, occasional punishments, and some involvement	Motivation is based on compensation system developed through participation

Source: Adapted from Likert (1967, Table 3, pp. 14–24).

Table 5.2. Productivity and dysfunctions relationship to management style.

	Management style			
	Exploitative authoritative	**Benevolent authoritative**	**Consultative**	**Participative**
Productivity	Mediocre	Fair to good	Good	Excellent
Excessive absence and turnover	Relatively high when people are allowed to move	Moderately high when people are allowed to move	Moderate	Low
Scrap loss and waste	Relatively high unless policed	Moderately high unless policed	Moderate	Low

Source: Adapted from Likert (1967, p. 24).

In his research, Likert found that participative management is the most effective (see Table 5.2 for the summary of his findings). However, participatory management can take 3 years of change work for an organization. Most organizations gave up before the goal was reached.

SEAM's goal is to develop participative management in organizations through the three axes of the SEAM process — intervention, teaching managers management tools, and coaching. When workers are allowed to participate in improving their workplace, they take an ownership of their work and the workplace thrives. Employees' participation is essential for effective organizations.

Likert also found that it is difficult to get accurate information about what is happening in an organization.

> All levels of hierarchy in an organization, except the very top, fear measurements which are used in a punitive a manner by their superiors. To protect themselves they tend to resist covertly, if not overtly, the collection of such data. They also try, and often successfully, to distort the measurements in ways to favor or protect themselves. (p. 134)

We found the same in SEAM interventions. During data collection, the first instinct of employees is to say that there are not many wrong things. Employees fear that things that do not work might show them in a bad light. Two feedback sessions, the Mirror Effect and the Expert Opinion, start changing employees' attitude to data. Employees see that real problems are identified and no one is blamed, hurt, or fired. As they gain confidence and trust in the intervention process, they begin to talk about what does not work in the organization. Realization that talking about dysfunctions is safe improves the flow of information, both upward and downward.

Douglas MacGregor (1906–1964). Douglas McGregor was American social psychologist and management professor. He proposed that managers' assumptions about human nature and behavior shaped how they managed employees. In *The Human Side of Enterprise* (1985), he described two sets of these assumptions, which he titled Theory X and Theory Y. Here is a summary of how McGregor described the two theories:

Theory X assumptions:

- Management's role is to coerce and control employees.
- The average human being has an inherent dislike of work and will avoid it if he can.
- Because of this human characteristic of dislike of work, most people must be coerced, controlled, directed, and threatened with punishment to get them to put forth adequate effort toward the achievement of organizational objectives.
- The average human being prefers to be directed, does not want responsibility, has relatively little ambition, and wants security above all else (pp. 33–34).

Theory Y assumptions:

- Management's role is to develop the potential in employees and help them to release that potential toward common goals.
- The expenditure of physical and mental effort in work is as natural as play or rest.

- External control and the threat of punishment are not the only means to bring about effort toward organizational objectives. Man will exercise self-direction and self-control in the service of objectives to which he is committed.
- Commitment to objectives is a function of the rewards associated with their achievement. The most significant of such rewards, e.g., the satisfaction of the ego and self-actualization needs, can be direct products of effort directed toward organizational objectives.
- The average human being learns, under proper conditions, not only to accept but to seek responsibility.
- The capacity to exercise a relatively high degree of imagination, ingenuity, and creativity in the solution of organizational problems is widely, not narrowly, distributed in the human population.
- Under the conditions of modern industrial life, the intellectual potentialities of the average human being are only partly utilized (pp. 47–48).

SEAM is based on the assumptions about a human being that are very close to the Theory Y assumptions. In fact, the stress on the development of human potential is perfectly aligned with Theory Y. The intervention process, training of managers, and coaching leaders are designed to foster a Theory Y workplace.

Chris Argyris (1923–2013). Chris Argyris, an American social psychologist, developed the concepts of the ladder of inference, theories-in-use, single- and double-loop learning, and the learning organization. His teachings were also influential on the development of socio-economic theory.

The ladder of inference is the concept that describes people's thinking processes when they draw incorrect conclusions about facts or events. This thinking is usually done automatically without people being consciously aware of steps in their chain of logic. The implication of this concept is twofold. The first implication is the very process of climbing the ladder of inferences. Between the first step of seeing, hearing, or experiencing something and the final step of responding to this

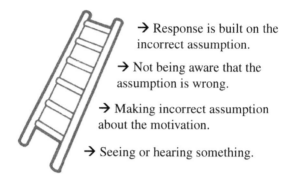

→ Response is built on the incorrect assumption.

→ Not being aware that the assumption is wrong.

→ Making incorrect assumption about the motivation.

→ Seeing or hearing something.

Figure 5.2.   Climbing the ladder of inference.

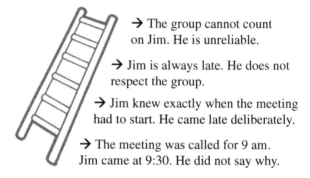

→ The group cannot count on Jim. He is unreliable.

→ Jim is always late. He does not respect the group.

→ Jim knew exactly when the meeting had to start. He came late deliberately.

→ The meeting was called for 9 am. Jim came at 9:30. He did not say why.

Figure 5.3.   An example of climbing the ladder of inference by a work group.

stimulus, people go through a series of assumptions. These assumptions may be absolutely incorrect, but people are not aware of them (see Figure 5.2).

Figure 5.3 presents an example of climbing the ladder of inference. A group made a series of assumptions based on the fact of a group member being late, and the response will be the changes in the group's attitude and behavior of their colleague.

Climbing the ladder of inference is a frequent problem in organizations. The results of using the ladder of inference are miscommunication, poor understanding, and mistrust between actors, which undermine their cooperation.

The second implication of the ladder of inference is that people select which "facts" to observe, and then they interpret these "facts" through the filter of what they think is true and objective. When people climb the ladder of inference, they base their thinking on the following tacit assumptions:

- My beliefs are the truth.
- My truth is objective and obvious.
- I base my beliefs on real data.
- The data I select are real data.

The result of the ladder of inference is a biased viewpoint that people imagine to be objective reality. However, the reality can be so complex, especially when it comes to a socially constructed reality, that different perspectives not only can be valid and correct, they can also be contradictory. When people are not aware of their assumptions about truth, they are not able to listen to anything that does not fit their picture of reality that leads to conflict.

SEAM has a concept that is similar to the ladder of inference, "contradictory inter-subjectivity," which refers to the fact that actors see reality differently, based on their assumptions and beliefs. All actors' viewpoints are "subjective" and shaped by their "internal" lens; some of the viewpoints may "contradict" each other, and this is why the term is contradictory inter-subjectivity. The fact that different actors will see the situation differently is considered in the diagnostic phase of intervention. When intervener-researchers collect data, they are not trying to discover the exact truth. They ignore discrepancies between participants' viewpoints, since each person will climb his or her own ladder of inference. The Mirror Effect session usually clarifies some of the misunderstandings, and the group creates its own sense of organizational reality based on the data fed back to them by the intervener-researchers.

The ladder of inference and contradictory inter-subjectivity echo the teaching of Perroux, who argued that researchers are never neutral, as they interpret facts through their own lens of reality.

Single- and double-loop learning. While working with organizations, Argyris noticed that people were often unable to detect and correct their mistakes, which impaired people's learning. To explain people's inability to learn, Argyris came up with the concepts of single-loop and double-loop learning. Single-loop learning happens when in encountering a problem, one's response is only to change the actions that led to the problem. For example, if a cook discovered that his dish was too salty, then the next time he made the dish, he would add less salt. In Argyris's language, single-loop learning occurs when a mismatch in a person's behavior and intention is detected, and the correction of the error happens without changing the person's underlying beliefs or assumptions.

However, when the problem is the result of the governing beliefs, in other words, people's beliefs or assumptions, then single-loop learning will not fix the problem. This is the time for double-loop learning, which calls for examining the underlying assumptions that led to the action. Using Argyris' language, double-loop learning occurs when a mismatch in a person's behavior and intention is detected and corrected by changing one's governing beliefs (see Figure 5.4).

For example, an organization repeatedly asks its employees to be more proactive with new initiatives about how to expand. Employees are not eager to do so, as they are afraid to be blamed and punished in the case of failure. Until the organization changes its governing belief that failures and mistakes must result in punishment of those at fault, it will be hard to change employees' behavior and make them be proactive in taking risks.

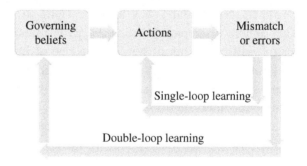

Figure 5.4. Single- and double-loop learning.

While double-loop learning looks like an effective tool to make people and organizations change, it seems simple in theory. In practice, it may be difficult to identify certain beliefs and assumptions that lead to undesired practices. One has to be courageous and self-reflective enough to undertake the exploration. It can also be difficult to change those beliefs after they are identified due to lack of skills, guidance, or any other internal and external factors.

SEAM interventions foster double-loop learning of employees and the organization. Changing beliefs can happen in two ways. One is when an actor hears about a different way of believing, ponders the new idea, and adopts it. Another way is when an actor begins to follow a new model of behavior, and after a while adopts the belief that is the reasoning for the new behavior.

For example, one of the steps of the Expert Opinion is to identify the root causes of dysfunctions. The cause might be organizational practices (behaviors) or it might be the actors' attitudes (assumptions) that lead to those practices. The actors may or may not be ready or able to analyze their underlying assumptions behind the practices. However, they are able to identify behaviors they want to change, and after they change the behaviors, they might realize later that their attitudes and assumptions eventually changed too.

Here is an example to show that sometimes changing practices of behavior may inform the changing belief system. A manager wrote up her employees whenever they made a mistake. She believed that workers need to be punished for not obeying organizational rules. During the SEAM intervention, she was introduced to the SEAM beliefs about management and the SEAM management tools. She began to steer rather than to punish employees. Several months later, she confessed to having a different appreciation of employees and their roles and about her role as a supervisor. She also felt very relieved at not needing to punish employees every time something went wrong. In the beginning, she was not a very good supervisor. Both she and her reports disliked the punishments. In order for her to become a better supervisor, she had to go through double-loop learning. It took time, but in the end, the new practice led to the change in her governing beliefs about what makes a good manager.

Theory of action and theory-in-use. Argyris wrote about two different sets of beliefs that guide people's behavior under the risk of embarrassment or threat. Argyris called them theories of action and theories-in-use. Theory of action is what people espouse, or what they say to others about their actions. Theory-in-use is the conscious and unconscious beliefs that shape people's actual behavior.

There is a common saying, "this person does not walk the talk," which means the person says one thing but acts in a way that contradicts the words. In Argyris's language, this person has a gap between the espoused theory of action and the actual theory-in-use. Organizations can also have a gap between theory of action and theory-in use. For example, many organizations espouse the idea, "Our employees are our most valuable asset." However, in the time of crisis, employees become the first commodity to dispose. Or a manager may say that he respects and values his employees while his employees may experience his style to be very disrespectful. Usually, people are not aware that what they say about their actions and how they act are not in sync. Argyris argued that one's effectiveness comes from developing the congruence of one's espoused theory and theory-in-use.

Model 1 theory-in-use. A theory-in-use is a set of tacit beliefs that drive actual behavior; Argyris called them the master programs. People use these master programs to be in control when they perceive an embarrassment or threat to their competence, power, or self-image. In studying his participants, Argyris found that most people operate from the Model 1 theory-in-use. The governing beliefs of people who operate in Model 1 theory-in-use are as follows:

1. To win
2. To stay in unilateral control
3. To suppress negative feelings

The problem with Model 1 theory-in-use is that it is not workable. To be effective, the holder of Model 1 theory-in-use needs to work with people who have differing beliefs or desires or a different theory-in-use. At the same time, most people will have the same urges to win, be in control, and to suppress negative feelings. It is impossible to always win and to completely repress all negative feelings in the people who always lose.

Organizational defensive routines. In organizations that operate from Model 1 theory-in-use, the tension between winning and avoiding negative feelings is resolved by what Argyris called organizational defensive routines. These are the defensive mechanisms by which people cover up and deny that there is any discrepancy between their espoused values and their actual behavior. Argyris described organizational defensive routines as actions or policies that prevent individuals from experiencing embarrassment or threat and also from identifying and getting rid of the causes of potential embarrassment or threat. People become very skilled at covering up issues that might be embarrassing or threatening and they are not aware of doing so. The skill becomes an automatic reaction, rather than a process that is thought through.

Organizational defensive routines become the normative behaviors in the workplace. One of the defensive routines is fancy footwork, in which everybody becomes blind to their self-deception. Here is an example of fancy footwork. In a medical clinic, the staff espoused that their top priority was providing excellent care for all patients. At the same time, numerous dysfunctions reduced the time that the physicians had to see patients. Although the physicians had a scheduled amount of time to see each patient, the actual time of the visit was 30–50% less. The reduced amount of time of the physician–patient visit did not allow physicians to identify more serious medical issues in the patients. When faced with the issue of not spending allocated time with patients, all actors did not see this as a problem because they believed they still provided the best possible care. First, the actors were not aware (blind) that less time with a patient often affected the quality of the care. Second, they used fancy footwork to negate the connection between the amount of the time of the visit and the quality of care. Third, the actors blamed consultants for not understanding how hard they work and what good patient care they provide.

Model 2 theory-in-use. Argyris worked on helping people move from Model 1 to Model 2 theory-in-use, which is based on a different set of beliefs. Organizations or people will be most effective if they

1. Use valid (and validatable) information
2. Use free and informed choice
3. Have commitment to decisions, including constant monitoring of the decision's effectiveness

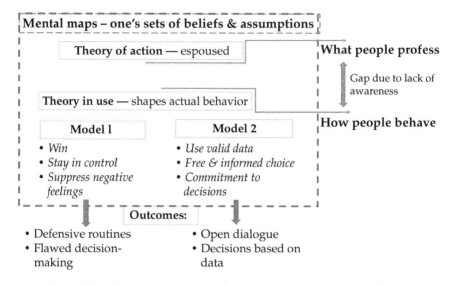

Figure 5.5.   Visual representation of Argyris's theories-in-action and in-use.

Model 2 calls for the use of good data and inclusion of knowledge and experiences of those who are involved. When a group operates by using Model 2 theory-in-use, the group becomes open to exploring ideas and making sure that decisions are made based on data and without coercion. Model 2 is conducive to double-loop learning and for the development of a learning organization.

Problems of the workplace. In his early research, Argyris focused on the impact of formal organizational structures, control systems, and management on individuals, in particular, how people responded and adapted to management systems. Some of his findings were published in the book *Integrating the Individual and the Organization* (1990, originally published in 1964). This is what Argyris wrote about the workplace:

1. Work is highly specialized and fractionalized: It is broken down to the simplest possible motions. The assumption is that the easier the work, (a) the more the productivity, (b) the less the training time needed, (c) the greater the flexibility for the interchangeability of the worker, and (d) the greater the satisfaction of the employee because the less the frustration and/or responsibility that he will intend to experience.

2. Responsibility for the planning of work for defining production rates and for maintaining control over speed is placed in the hands of management but not in the hands of those doing the actual producing of the product.
3. Responsibility for issuing orders, changing work, shifting employees, indeed for the most important changes in the worker's world is also invested in top management.
4. Responsibility for evaluating performance and for developing and disbursing of rewards and penalties lies primarily in the hands of management.
5. Responsibility for deciding who may remain, who must leave, and when these decisions shall be made is also vested in the management of the organization (p. 37).

Argyris outlined three consequences of this style of management. One outcome is, few of a worker's abilities will be used. In other words, the worker's human potential will not be tapped. The second outcome is, workers will develop feelings of dependence and submissiveness toward their superiors. The third outcome is, workers' sense of self-responsibility and self-control will be reduced.

What Argyris described sounds like the forerunner of the TFW virus metaphor. Work is fragmented, workers are obedient, and managers make all the workplace decisions. Workers' self-esteem and commitment are damaged.

The foundational elements of SEAM include developing human potential, using the knowledge and skills of workers to solve workplace dysfunctions and reducing the blindness caused by the virus and organizational defensive routines. Each of these is in harmony with Argyris's research about the effective workplace.

Learning organizations. The essence of being a learning organization is having practices that lead employees to be open to listening and learning. This implies the organization must reward openness and truth telling. Argyris described four steps to help an organization become a learning organization, in other words, an organization with the capacity to learn, especially when the organization deals with issues that are embarrassing or threatening:

1. Map how the organization deals with problems.
2. Help individuals diagnose how they contribute to the current method of problem-solving.
3. Reeducate people to use Model 2, moving them from espoused Model 2 values to action, which is based on Model 2 values, i.e., make Model 2 their theory-in-use.
4. Repeat the learning experience to solve new problems.

His method is similar to the SEAM intervention process: using the Mirror Effect to identify problems, identifying unspoken causes for dysfunctions, and creating the opportunity for actors to solve the old problems and later new problems as they arise.

Savall cited Argyris in his books, *Work and People: An Economic Evaluation of Job-Enrichment, The Qualimetrics Approach: Observing the Complex Object,* and *The Dynamics and Challenges of Tetranormalization,* indicating that Argyris did influence Savall's thinking. Argyris' Model 2 theory-in-use is implicit in the SEAM workplace.

Use valid (and validatable) information. The Mirror Effect and Expert Opinion provide information to all actors. The data are validated by actors during the Mirror Effect. In addition, the values of the hidden costs in an organization are data that most organizations do not have, which weakens the leadership's ability to make decisions.

Use free and informed choice. Many actors are afraid to speak up when they have information or opinions that they believe managers will not like. Sometimes their reticence comes from their experience in the organization. Sometimes managers are open, but actors carry their reticence based on previous experiences. The SEAM process is designed to help actors learn to communicate without fear. Having leaders undergo the Mirror Effect and Expert Opinion before others in the organization provide a chance for leaders to model openness to discomforting information without assigning blame. The SEAM notion that dysfunctions are a problem of the system, and not of individuals, reinforces the need to fix the system rather than blame the individual actor.

Have commitment to decisions, including constant monitoring of the effectiveness of the decisions. The purpose of the Piloting LogBook management tool is to measure the effect of the improvement projects and to monitor the effectiveness of the decisions made by the group. If the decision needs to be revisited, the group decides what data have to be used. Through the projects, the group members learn the Model 2 behaviors and eventually model those behaviors to the rest of the organization.

Summary

Socio-economic theory is built on the intersection of multiple disciplines and critical assessment of different theories and scholarly work. Savall was influenced by two major disciplines — economics of the 20th century and Northern American and European OD. Savall drew heavily on the economic and ethical works of the Spanish and French authors, Bernácer and Perroux. Their concept of the importance of developing human potential is at the heart of SEAM. Treating every actor with respect in the workplace is both most effective for the organization's success and morally right.

The field of OD influenced the socio-economic theory through the work of authors such as Lewin, MacGregor, and Likert. Their ideas can be seen in the highly participative approach to the workplace that is core to SEAM. Hertzberg influenced Savall's understanding of what motivates workers. The writings of Argyris added another dimension: How to make people in organizations change the unconscious beliefs that shape their behaviors, which in turn lead to organizational dysfunctions. While being influenced by social sciences and economics, Savall was able to integrate social, economic, and financial elements of different disciplines in developing and applying his socio-economic theory.

Chapter 6

Organizational Problems and How SEAM Can Help

In our consulting work with organizations, we run into many common problems of the modern workplace. Some of them may be unique to a specific organization, but many problems are the same regardless of the organizational type, size, or nature of the industry. These problems are caused by the Taylorism, Fayolism, Weberism (TFW) virus, and thus we use the socio-economic approach to management (SEAM) lens to help organizations recognize and resolve the problematic issues. In this chapter, we explore two of the most common organizational problems that are often under the organizational radar and show how SEAM helps with each of these problems.

Magical Thinking as Organizational Dysfunction

Time is perhaps the only resource that cannot be replenished. Frequently, employees of different ranks say that they have too much work and too little time to complete the work. They go on to explain, "If only I had enough time, then I would be able to get everything done." As a result, they feel stressed and hopeless. They believe they are failing at being good employees, and some become depressed and burnout. They see the source of this problem as not having enough time to do all the works they need to do.

However, the real problem is that these people have a delusional belief that they can do more work than they actually can do. We coined the term "Magical thinking" to explain to people that often their thinking is the source of their problems. Magical thinking is a delusional belief that one can do the impossible. Magical thinking is very common in the modern workplace and is harmful to employees and destructive of organizational productivity and efficiency.

For example, one of the forms of magical thinking is people's delusion about the amount of work they can do in a certain unit of time. When people are asked to do more than they can actually do, the normal response would be "That is not possible." People may then attempt to fulfill the request, but they do not feel undue anxiety when they fail. What has been surprising is that people in the workplace frequently become stressed and anxious because of their inability to do what rationally they know they cannot do.

The stress and anxiety from not being able to do an unrealistic amount of work is the result of being infected by the TFW virus. In fact, this situation is a good example of how people are not aware that they hold flawed assumptions about work. The TFW virus is a metaphor for the dominant set of beliefs about people, work, and workplace (see Chapter 2). The TFW virus has been spread through business schools in the Western world and shaped the normative mental model about business and management; yet even people without management training have been infected by the virus. When people are not aware of the TFW virus, they can develop a neurosis that has the potential to lead to physical and mental illnesses.

Magical Thinking as a Form of Neurosis

Carl Jung, a Swiss psychologist and the founder of analytical psychology, used the term "neurosis" to describe the internal process in which an unconscious conflict creates anxiety. According to Jung, the ego is the center of conscious awareness. The internal task of the ego is to bring the conscious and unconscious aspects of the mind into a workable harmony. If the ego fails to integrate the elements of conscious and unconscious, the result is that one has a poor ability to adapt to one's environment and change one's life patterns (see Figure 6.1).

Ego's task:
To bring the conscious
and unconscious
aspects of the mind
into a workable
harmony

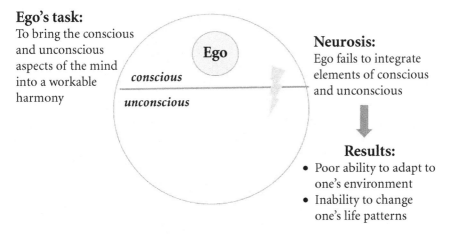

Neurosis:
Ego fails to integrate
elements of conscious
and unconscious

Results:
• Poor ability to adapt to
one's environment
• Inability to change
one's life patterns

Figure 6.1.   Jung's concept of neurosis.

Everyone has, at some point in life, some unconscious unresolved conflicts. What matters is whether this conflict is resolved in a healthy way, or whether unresolved conflict leads to anxiety and/or depression that can affect one's mental and physical health. The term "neurosis" is used here to define the unresolved inner conflict which is severe enough to threaten one's mental and/or physical health.

Here is an example to convey the point. When a person has more tasks to do than what one can reasonably complete in a certain amount of time, and then two inner messages occur. One message is "I should do all the tasks," and the other message is "I cannot do all the tasks in the time allocated to do these tasks." A healthy resolution comes from the awareness of both sides of the tension and then making a choice, e.g., the person may choose not to do everything, or to try while accepting that failure is a strong possibility. A healthy resolution of the inner conflict happens when a person recognizes a tension between contradictory messages, makes a choice of action, then accepts the outcome of the action, and moves on (see Figure 6.2).

However, sometimes people think that they should do, or are being told to do, more than what they can accomplish. The TFW virus fosters the belief that employees really should be obedient to their bosses, and if they cannot measure up, then there is something wrong with the

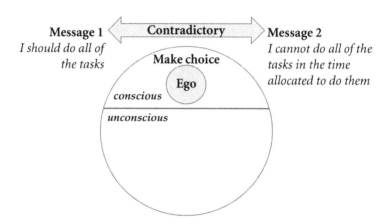

Figure 6.2.   Healthy resolution comes from recognizing the tension between contradictory messages and making a choice.

employees. People, infected by the TFW virus, accept the premise that doing the impossible can be done and thus should be done. At this point, the second side of the inner tension, which is "I cannot do all the work," is repressed and buried in the unconscious. It is easier for the person to bury the awareness that she cannot do the work, rather than to admit that she cannot do it. The reasons can be various — saving face, pleasing the boss, wanting praise or recognition, etc. Now, there are two contradictory messages on the unconscious level — "not being able to do more work" and "doing impossible things is possible," which lead to unconscious tension and thus neurosis (see Figure 6.3).

The unresolved inner tensions may lead to anxiety, depression, and overwork, which in turn lead to burnout and/or depersonalization. In our practice, we have often seen people with each of these symptoms that were caused by their magical thinking that they could do the impossible.

Types of Magical Thinking

While theoretically everybody would agree that magical thinking is not effective, many smart and reasonable people do not notice how they fall

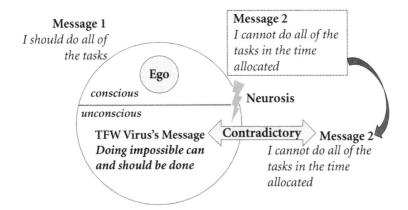

Figure 6.3.   Unhealthy resolution is burying a contradictory message in the unconscious, which in turn creates an unconscious tension with already existing unconscious assumption of the TFW virus.

into the trap of magical thinking. Below are some examples of the most common and frequently used types of magical thinking that exist in organizations.

Doing more with less will not affect quality. There is a common business practice of committing to doing more with less resources, believing that this can be done without reducing quality. Many are familiar with the phrase, "Work smarter not harder." While this might be appropriate at times, there is a limit that needs to be recognized. The reasons to do more with less are often noble. An organization's students, or patients, or clients are very important and so the organization has to keep providing services, even when there are less people or resources to do the work. The fact that doing more with less will inevitably lead to lower quality is usually not discussed or is absolutely denied.

We often see people, especially those who are good in what they are doing, get burdened with more workload, which they cannot possibly complete. We have seen people carrying the work of two, or even three employees, because there is no one else to pick up the tasks. Common sense dictates that it is not possible to do three jobs without impacting the quality of the jobs. As a result, many projects are not finished 100%. The sense of "the project is good enough" and knowing that there are many other projects waiting leads people to move on to another project. But uncompleted work will turn later into major dysfunctions and eventually will lead to extra work and dissatisfaction from the clients.

Some psychological consequences to doing more with less include a Martyr complex in employees. Martyrs sacrifice self, rescuing or supporting others because of an unconscious need for validation by others. People with a martyr complex tend to believe that they are serving others well, even at the cost of their own health and development. When they are not validated enough, they may use guilt to try to manipulate others. Asking martyrs to do the impossible can feed the unconscious needs of martyrs, making magical thinking almost inevitable.

Interruptions are an unavoidable part of work. Not addressing the interruptions that eat away at one's productivity is another form of magical thinking. Interruptions can be as simple as the continuous checking of email at each time when there is a notification of a new message. Interruptions can also come from continuous phone calls that prevent one from doing work that requires much concentration, or from people stopping by to ask a work-related question or just to say hello. The dysfunction is very sneaky, as the interruptions do not seem like a serious problem, yet they eat up a lot of time and reduce people's focus and effectiveness. When an interruption happens, people, who were doing a task, have to focus on a different issue, and then to refocus on the previous task. The time needed to get back on task is the dysfunction. It may take 30 seconds to 5 minutes per interruption, but when there are many interruptions in a day, one can see a significant loss of time and effectiveness.

When people are told that having too many or unnecessary interruptions are dysfunctional, their first reaction is that interruptions are part of work. After people recognize the fact that interruptions are an issue, they argue that the interruptions are inevitable and nothing can be done to change them. Both reactions are examples of blindness, which is one of the symptoms of the TFW virus. In one office of seven people, we measured the hidden cost of crisis phone calls that continuously rang and did not allow any member of the group to focus for more than a few minutes. The value of time wasted on interruptions was estimated at $60,000 per year, in addition to the stress that employees felt. After a reorganization of duties, they were able to reduce the hidden cost by one-third.

Newly promoted supervisors will know how to manage without supervisory training. Another type of magical thinking is promoting employees to supervisory positions without providing a proper training in how to manage people. It goes without saying that one needs knowledge and skills to be a good supervisor, and it is unrealistic to expect a newly promoted employee to be a good supervisor without prior experience or training. Expecting that newly appointed supervisors will automatically know how to supervise people is magical thinking that can be found in many organizations.

This type of magical thinking is aggravated by not removing some of the prior duties from newly promoted supervisors' job expectations. When newly promoted supervisors are not trained to be supervisors, they do not learn that they have to spend part of their time managing, or steering, the employees who report to them. The supervisors now face two tasks: supervising, which is a mystery to them and does not seem to be valued by management, and doing all of the operational works, they did before, and which were previously the sources of job satisfaction. As a result, under the time pressure, they tend to spend their time in operations not supervision. Although they acquired the new management responsibilities, they did not develop a mindset of being a manager. Many organizations have fallen into this type of magical thinking, and then leaders wonder why their employees have low morale or decide to leave.

Steering the organizational ship does not take much time. Leading an organization is like steering a ship. Not putting enough time into steering but expecting the organization to meet its strategic goals successfully is another type of magical thinking that is found among an organization's top leaders. Steering includes aligning people and resources, synchronizing the work of different silos so that their efforts are in accordance with the organizational mission and strategic goals, and developing the potential of employees. The socio-economic theory suggests that steering the organization is the primary task of top managers. In fact, lack of steering is one of the five root causes of all organizational dysfunctions (see more on root causes in Chapter 2).

Lack of steering may take different forms. The most obvious form is when an organization does not have a clear direction. This may happen when not all leaders agree on or have a clear picture of the organizational mission or strategic plan. In our work with top leaders, we often heard that the leaders knew the mission, yet upon further exploration, it became clear that the leaders had a different interpretation of the mission or a different understanding of how to fulfill the mission. The lack of agreement on mission and strategic plan led to competition to reach different goals. The top leaders had different assumptions about the strategic direction of the organization, and so their departments were not aligned. A variation on this lack of steering happens when leaders do activities and undertake initiatives that are not part of the organization's strategic plan. The metaphorical description for this situation is a strategic plan that sits on a shelf while the organization wanders aimlessly.

Another form of lack of steering is when top leaders, instead of thinking strategically and systemwide, get caught up in micromanaging. They look closely at the minutia and miss the big picture. At one organization, the top leaders would weekly review all expenditures in the multi-million-dollar budget. They spent so much time and energy on the budget review that they were not able to steer — to align the work of all the departments in the organization. As a result, departments worked in isolation, which caused many dysfunctions.

When leaders are not trained to think systemically, they focus only on their own division, rather than on how the whole system is affected by what happens in their division. Not seeing the big picture and burying oneself into operational activities can lead to the lack of synchronization of different silos and turf wars. An example of turf wars can be seen in budgeting. Top leaders may hoard their portion of the budget, regardless of the needs of other parts of the organization. The lack of steering leads to the lack of synchronization and the organization as a whole pays the price. Good steering implies assessing the needs of the whole organization and realigning the budget to best meet the organizational mission.

To summarize, magical thinking is alive and well in the workplace and is the result of the TFW virus. Magical thinking can cause stress and anxiety, can lead to a feeling of failure or hopelessness, and can lead to burnout and neurosis. From our experience, magical thinking is causing a great number of organizational dysfunctions and negatively impacts people and their wellbeing in the workplace.

SEAM as an Antidote to Magical Thinking

As part of a SEAM intervention, all managers are taught to use the SEAM management tools. While more information on tools is presented in Chapter 4, here we only describe how tools work for reducing magical thinking about time.

The Time Management tool helps managers to assess the use of their time. Each manager keeps a log of what they do over several typical days. The important characteristic of the SEAM Time Management tool is that it distinguishes the time spent on activities that are the result of dysfunctions. Managers examine how much time was spent within the following categories:

- Doing routine management duties
- Doing the work of people at a lower pay scale
- Responding to organizational dysfunctions
- Preventing dysfunctions
- Steering direct reports

Usually, this is the first tool that SEAM intervener–researchers introduce, so from the very beginning of the intervention, managers start thinking about how they use their time. They become more respectful of their time. As one IT supervisor told us, "I used to jump into task right away, regardless of who asked me do it. Now I am thinking twice before I do something because I do not want to waste my time on dysfunctions. The Time Management tool taught me to respect my time."

The Internal/External Strategic Action Plan document lists the strategic goals to be achieved and includes both the goals for development or the external plans and the goals for reducing dysfunctions or the internal plans. The plan is for 3–5 years, and it outlines the objectives to be achieved within 6-month blocks of time and identifies the employees responsible for achieving the goals.

The Internal/External Strategic Action Plan prepares managers to do their Priority Action Plans. From the Internal/External Strategic Action Plan, everyone can see the goals set for the next 6 months. The task of each manager is to create a table, in which they include the internal and external goals. The managers also have to add their routine management duties and vacation, as well as the estimation of the time needed to deal with emergencies. This last piece is especially good for preventing magical thinking, as often organizations do not take into account that everyday activities and emergencies may eat up a lot of time, not leaving enough time for development and strategic planning.

The next step for managers is to estimate the amount of time needed to complete each of the tasks on their Priority Action Plan. To date, everyone with whom we have worked has found that they did not have enough time to be successful in all their tasks. One executive admitted, "Only after completing the Priority Action Plan did I realize that I won't be able to complete this project by the end of this year. In fact, I can see that I will not be able to start it sooner than the second part of the next year." This tool allowed the executive to become aware of his magical thinking in regard to what could be completed.

After all tools are completed and synchronized, managers have to meet with their bosses and negotiate how they will spend their time and on what activities. As a result, managers begin to view their time, capacity, and plans realistically, rather than succumb to magical thinking.

The Competency Grid reduces magical thinking about promoting supervisors without training them. In the Competency Grid, the department members list all of the knowledge and skills needed to complete their work successfully, as well as what skills need to be developed for future work. The skills of being a supervisor, such as interpersonal, conflict management, and communication skills, are included in the grid. The next step is assessing the extent to which each employee has mastery of the knowledge and skills, and which skills the employees would like to develop in the future. The recognition of the supervisory skills that are needed to be a good supervisor leads to a much more plan-full approach to developing supervisors' knowledge and skills and to robust succession planning.

While the Competency Grid may seem obvious, in our experience, many organizations are not spending the time to assess needed competencies, including those of supervisors and leaders. In fact, often after completing the competency grid, people say to us, "Where were you with this tool X months ago, when we were hiring in our division? Now we would

Table 6.1.   Types of magical thinking in organizations and possible remedies.

Types of magical thinking in organizations	SEAM elements as possible remedies
Doing more with less will not affect quality	Using the Time Management tool and Priority Action Plans; analysis of hidden costs; coaching
Adding more work without removing any tasks or adding more time will not affect quality	Using the Time Management tool, Internal/External Strategic Action Plan, and Priority Action Plans
Interruptions are an unavoidable part of work	Using the Time Management tool; analysis of hidden costs
Newly promoted supervisors will know how to manage, without supervisory training	Training managers; coaching; using the competency grid and Priority Action Plans
Steering the organizational ship does not take much time	Using Priority Action Plans; coaching; fostering strategic and systems thinking

hire a person with a totally different set of skills, the one that our division needs the most." Table 6.1 summarizes the types of magical thinking and the SEAM elements that reduce its impact.

The intent was to name the phenomenon of magical thinking and to show some of the ways in which the SEAM management tools work to counteract the neurotic behaviors that are result of the TFW virus. The reader may look for other examples of magical thinking and ponder on ways to reduce those. Whatever the methods are used to address, reduce, or eliminate magical thinking, the result will be the increased organizational efficiency, and a healthier and more joyous workplace.

Dysfunctional Implementation of Initiatives

For years, there have been debates about the reasons and number of failures of organizational change and business initiatives. Numerous business articles, books, and online blogs have been written that describe six, ten, or many "Main reasons" why strategic plans or change initiatives fail. Most of those reasons are common sense, at least for practitioners who work in organization development and change management. In terms of numbers, the opinions differ. Some claim that somewhere between 60% and 90% of change efforts and business initiatives fail to meet their objectives, while others argue that the rate of failure is lower. Regardless of the number, many organizations have certain practices that lead to failed initiatives. The following section explores the reasons behind failed initiatives and what is needed to implement the sustainable change.

Leaders' ideas are not translated into strategy. The first problem of failed implementation is the inability of the top leaders to translate ideas into strategy. The leaders have a great idea of an initiative and they talk about it a lot, yet the initiative remains to live at the level of ideas. There are several possible causes for the leaders' inability to transform ideas into strategy.

Inability to focus. The result of inability to translate thoughts into action is babble, ongoing talk about improvement that never leads to any outcomes. We call the failure to implement ideas into action as a Tower of Babble (pun intended) for two reasons. First, the people at different organizational levels rarely talk the same language and have a different understanding about their organization's mission, strategy, and tactics. Second, a lot of energy is spent on talking. This is ironic because when being asked about the biggest problem in the organizations, employees often respond that there is not enough communication. So, people talk a lot, but they neither hear nor act. As in the old saying about railroad loco-motives, all the steam goes into the whistle. None of the steam produces movement.

Short lifespan of an idea. We worked with some leadership teams who could easily generate new ideas. After several months of talking about how to implement an idea, they dropped the idea and moved on to another idea. Sometimes, the ideas would get to the phase of implementation and, not getting any support, die. This approach is common in some business environments and has a name — the shiny object syn-drome. Chasing new shiny objects may cost organizations hundreds of thousands of dollars in wasted time, resources, and missed productivity. In additional to hidden costs in the form of wasted resources and time, chasing a new shiny object has the risk of lowering morale and reducing employee engagement. In one organization, when we spoke to employees about how they understood the organizational strategy and how they aligned their work with it, one worker said, "The organizational strategy changes all the time. The leadership constantly chases a new shiny object. I do not know where we are going any more. So why bother?" Employees lose trust in leadership and believe that nothing can improve the organization. The ideas for the leadership come and go, the reality for employees remains as before. They are hopeless that their work will ever improve.

Ineffective decision-making. One of the signs of effective leadership teams is the ability to make sound decisions, based on data, in a timely manner. Yet, in some leadership teams, the members are not able to disagree; the members fear the leader or others in the group, so hold back their thoughts. As a result, the business discussions in those groups turn into a politically correct dance without talking about the real issues. We worked with one executive group, in which the CEO dominated every meeting and was notorious for retaliating against anyone who did not agree with him. As a result, the group learned to defer to the CEO, watched carefully for his opinions and reactions, and withheld any information that would displease him. Therefore, the CEO never had full and accurate information about what was happening in the organization. The team members had to talk in private about what was troublesome or important and often tried to filter any information for the leader in order not to upset him.

In some leadership teams, even if the members could talk about the real issues, they simply could not make sound decisions in a timely manner. We have seen teams of good, caring, smart leaders, who talked and talked and talked, but were not able to reach actual decisions. When we asked them why this happens, the leaders had different excuses, such as the need to collect more information or to test the ideas, fear to make the wrong decision, or desire to make a perfect decision. Yet the perfect decision is the one that is made with all the information available at the time and communicated in a timely manner to everyone involved in the decision. As time goes by, the decision should be revisited and adjusted if needed, based on the new information.

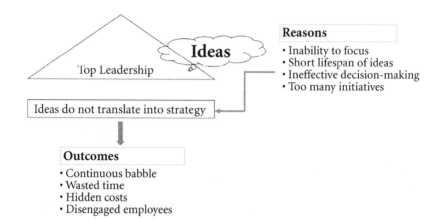

Figure 6.4. The problem of failed initiatives when top leaders' ideas are not translated into strategy.

Not knowing or ignoring the difference of personal styles may also lead to poor decision-making. We worked with teams, in which the leader, who was highly "Perceiving" in the Myers-Briggs typology, preferred gathering ideas rather than making decisions and so was continually tempted to wait for more information. Although collecting more information to make a sound decision is not a problem in itself, it may be very frustrating for those who are ready to decide. Inability to decide in a timely manner, or at least to talk openly about this issue, may lead to the loss of a momentum needed for implementation.

Too many initiatives. Another reason for leaders' inability to translate ideas into a strategy is that they are often overwhelmed by other tasks. These leaders have been caught by magical thinking in believing they can keep adding tasks to their work to-do lists without lowering the quality of their work. While there are different forms of magical thinking, being unrealistic about the relationship between time and work amount is one of the most common work place problems that lead to huge hidden costs.

Strategy is not translated into effective action. When leaders do manage to translate their ideas into strategy, there are several possible limiting factors to successful implementation at both top and middle management levels.

Not enough time for implementation. Even the best initiative needs enough time to be properly implemented. It is similar to planting a seed — the seed needs to root, sprout, and grow to be a viable plant. The SEAM research shows that while the first significant improvements and results can be achieved within the first 3 months of the intervention, many more sustainable changes in culture and reduction of hidden costs are achieved by the end of the first year. Then the changes strengthen steadily over time. Each year, the organization's return on investment grows. This timeline is in accordance with Likert's research on implementing participative management (see Chapter 5). Likert's point was that implementation of participative management, as the most effective type of management, would produce the best results after 3 years, but many organizations gave up before that time. Most American organizations are not patient and tend to be short-term-oriented.

Failure to give clear instructions. Sometimes leaders are not able to give clear instructions to those who are supposed to implement the plan, usually the middle managers. Talking about an idea is different from giving instructions about its implementation. One employee complained, "I get this email from my boss who says I have to implement this initiative, but I have no idea how to do this, and I do not know whom to ask." Even a clear instruction may be misunderstood due to various reasons and that can weaken implementation. Yet, when there are no clear instructions and no timeline, there is a high probability that an implementation will fail.

Not enough authority. Sometimes implementation is impaired because the person, who is supposed to lead the implementation, does not have the authority to act. This might be due to micromanagement from a higher manager, or it might simply be that nobody thought through what kind of authority the person in charge of implementation needs. We have seen many examples of managers asking people to complete tasks without giving them proper authority to do so. In one organization, a newly appointed project manager was supposed to manage numerous projects but did not have any authority over the people who worked on the projects. He could neither bring the necessary people together nor keep the people accountable for failing to meet the project deadlines. For successful implementation, the person in charge needs the authority to bring people together, make decisions, and get the desired changes to take root.

Lack of managerial skills. Earlier, we mentioned a common problem of promoting people to management roles without training them on how to supervise employees. Usually, these newly promoted managers neither know how to manage nor do invest enough time in their new role. Because of the lack of training, such managers may not know how to design the tactical steps needed to implement the initiative. When managers are unable to plan and steer their department, they cannot successfully implement any initiatives.

Being overwhelmed. Like top leaders, many mid-level managers and supervisors are overwhelmed by work, although being overwhelmed for them may take more severe forms. Some of the overwork is the result of their magical thinking and loyalty to their boss or organization. Sometimes, they are overwhelmed due to dysfunctions in their organization. New tasks are being continuously delegated to the mid-level managers and supervisors from top levels of the organization. Or when people leave the organization and are not replaced, the managers and supervisors add to their own workload the tasks of those who left. There is a common practice in many organizations, when employees do two or three jobs. As one supervisor said, "They keep adding more tasks to my plate and when I complain — they say, 'Work smarter not harder.' Now I am also doing a job of someone who was laid off. This is a pattern in our organization. They lay off people and then redistribute their work among us." These people are already failing to do the work they have. So, when implementing a new initiative is added to their plate, and nothing is taken away, there is neither the time nor the energy to work on a new initiative.

In addition to the outcomes of failed initiatives, reduced morale, and employee engagement, too much overwork can lead to burnout, which can cause significant emotional and physical damages to the person, and tremendous cost to the organization. As an example, in a rural healthcare organization, the estimated overall cost to the organization of a physician burning out is between $500,000 and $1,000,000.

Outcomes of failed initiatives. Whatever the cause of the failure to implement a new initiative, there are two possible unfortunate outcomes.

Premature death of an initiative. One possible outcome is the initiative dies after people try to work through the tangle of organizational dysfunctions. Along the way, the initiative creates havoc in people's busy lives, adds stress, and leads to more dysfunctions and hidden costs. The resources used during the short life span of the idea turn into hidden costs in the form of wasted time, wasted money, missed productivity, and reduced morale. The lost time and money could have been used more effectively in the areas that needed them most. People may gossip a bit about inept leadership and move on with their daily tasks. The leadership group shifts their attention to a new shiny object. The *status quo*, however dysfunctional, is restored for the time being until the vicious cycle begins again.

Unintended results. Another form of failure is when the initiative does get implemented, but the results are not what the organization originally intended to achieve. This can happen because the initiative is treated as a standalone event and not as a part of a larger organizational system. Over and over, we see situations in which the implementation of the initiative in one organizational silo does not take into account possible consequences in another silo, or the whole organization, which leads to more hidden costs. We call this approach a "Peep-hole vision." Imagine looking through an old-fashioned peep hole after somebody rang a door bell. Recollect how distorted the person behind the door looks and how little perspective is available when looking out. Many organizations have this limited view of how a new initiative interrelates and interacts with other organizational elements, such as vision, mission, and strategic directions.

Here is an example of a peep-hole vision. A college decided to recruit more international students. The marketing department received the task of producing a new marketing campaign to attract an international population. Several recruiters were sent abroad, mostly to countries of Eastern Europe, Asia, and the Middle East to recruit students. The college leaders were excited when more international students began to enroll. Initially, it looked like the college successfully implemented the strategic initiative of being more international. Then some problems started popping up.

The college, looking at the initiative through a peep-hole, did not recognize the need to provide a structure to support the implementation of the idea. Among the new international student population, there were many Muslim students, who needed prayer rooms, pre-prayer ablution facilities, and instructors who could understand the different cultural assumptions and values of the new student population. Muslim students

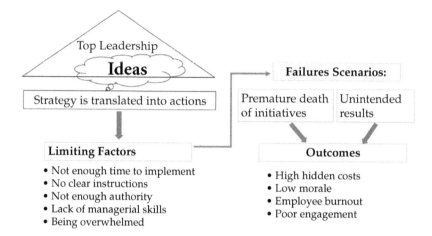

Figure 6.5. Limiting factors that prevent successful implementation of initiatives after the ideas are turned into strategies and tactics.

tried to resolve their needs on their own by using classrooms as the prayer rooms, washing feet before prayers in sinks and toilet bowls, and leaving class sessions at the hour of prayer, all of which caused frustration for other students and faculty. Conflict was escalated when some Muslim students went home and spread the word of mouth to not apply to the college. The college began to lose its international student population. This example illustrates the importance of looking at any initiative not as a single event, but something that has to be integrated into the whole system and then to be supported and maintained by the whole system.

What is needed for successful implementation of initiatives? While there are many causes for failed initiatives, there are only a few basic principles of successful implementation. In this book, SEAM is used as a lens to look at one method for implementing initiatives. However, there are other ways to implement change initiatives successfully. The underlying principles of all successful implementation processes are the same.

Support structures throughout the whole system. First, for an initiative or organizational change effort to be sustained, the implementation needs to include consideration of the impact on the whole system. If an initiative is implemented only in one silo, the other silos will have to support or maintain the change. This means that for successful implementation, the support structures have to be built throughout the whole system, regardless of what part of the system the initiative takes roots. The support structure for implementation includes procedures, polices, training, and feedback loops.

Using the right data. Second, every implementation needs to be grounded in sound data. The data should come from all levels of organization to provide a holistic picture of the state of things. The data should include not only the official numbers on financial sheets and other formal records, but also the hidden costs that are often ignored by traditional accounting. Usually, the hidden costs give a better picture of where implementation may stumble.

Training managers. Third, implementing a serious change in an organization often involves changing managers' behaviors, which may include changing their mental model of what the management entails. The primary task of managers is steering (getting all people and departments aligned) and setting the strategic direction for the organization. To set strategic direction and steer employees toward the strategic goals successfully, managers need to learn how to manage their time effectively, to give clear instructions, to delegate tasks and authority, and to provide timely feedback.

Allotting enough time to be able to see results. The common denominator for all requirements, mentioned above, is time. Time is needed to think through, to collect the right information, to train people, and to change their behavior. Giving enough time for a serious change initiative to take root is essential. We suggest 3 years ought to be the norm for a time frame for making serious organizational changes. As one Italian proverb says, between the idea and its implementation, many pairs of shoes are worn out.

How SEAM helps to sustain change initiatives. SEAM is very effective in helping to implement change initiatives. There are numbers to prove this — out of over 1,800 ISEOR interventions in the last 42 years,

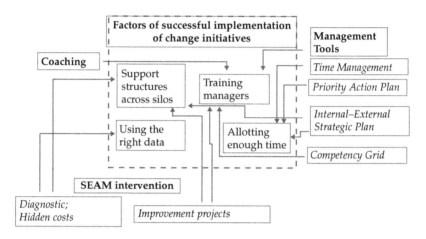

Figure 6.6.   The impact of different elements of the SEAM trihedron on the factors of successful implementation of change initiatives.

all but 2 were successfully implemented. The SEAM trihedron describes the change intervention, teaching managers to use the socio-economic management tools and coaching managers through the change efforts. Different elements of the SEAM trihedron impact the success of implementation (see Figure 6.6).

The SEAM intervention. The SEAM intervention is rigorous, data-driven, and theory-based. The goal of the intervention is to reduce organizational dysfunctions and hidden costs associated with them and increase human potential and engagement. The diagnostic phase of an improvement process provides leaders in every silo with an accurate information of what is not working well, and how much time and money the organization loses as a result. SEAM excels in gathering data from all levels of the organization, synthesizing data into specific categories, attaching a dollar amount to dysfunctions (hidden costs), and identifying the root causes of dysfunctions. Hidden costs information provides clear indicators of where a change initiative is needed. The improvement projects involve actors from all levels and departments that are affected by the project, which fosters an information exchange to help create successful change.

Management tools. The socio-economic management tools provide a disciplined way to successfully implement change. The tools serve as data gathering and negotiation tools. The tools, if used correctly, help to redirect the focus of intervention from blaming actors to addressing problems within the system. At first, people tend to be skeptical about tools, they may be even timid and assume that the tools will be used to reduce their freedom or, even worse, to jeopardize their work. However, later, when they discover all benefits of the tools, they realize how their life gets saner. The use of these management tools helps to rebuild a healthier and more effective system. When it comes to implementation of new initiatives, the SEAM management tools are helpful in allotting enough time needed for implementing initiatives and in aligning the efforts of different actors and silos with resources.

Coaching. Organizational change can be hard, as it upsets the strategic and political environment of the organization. One aspect of the coaching is helping leaders to deal with the political repercussions from the intervention process. As actors engage in reducing dysfunctions and creating a more collaborative workplace, they are inevitably changing "the rules of the game," i.e., the assumptions that people have about what is and is not acceptable at work. Ongoing coaching is extremely helpful for getting employees to live up to the new "rules," which in turn helps to sustain change.

Business case. Using an example is always helpful for understanding how theoretical concepts can be applied in practice. The following is a case of a real organization that dealt with some common and familiar problems.

The situation. In this organization, most managers and supervisors had more tasks than could be achieved, and they despaired of ever catching up. Everyone tried to work quickly, with the result that some things were missed. People understood that they needed to say "no" to something, but they did not know how to decide to what exactly they should say "no." The leadership group was unable to make decisions that lasted, so they wasted a tremendous amount of time by continually revisiting decisions. E-mail had become a crisis, and could eat up 1–4 hours a day for managers and supervisors. People recognized that they could not handle any more initiatives. One executive shared, "We have too many initiatives, without supporting, or educating people how to do them. We do not support, we just assign new projects to people." People became hopeless about ever changing anything. They accepted their fate.

The remedy. The interventions began with identifying dysfunctions and their causes. One of the problems identified in the diagnostic phase, was being overwhelmed, which was caused by the inability to manage time. Thus, the first step for the leadership group was to learn how to manage their time effectively.

The use of management tools. The Time Management tool led leaders to reflect on how much time they spent responding to dysfunctions, and how little time they spent steering the organization. As the leaders developed an Internal/External Strategic Action Plan, they faced the task of examining priorities that needed their attention for the next 3 years, as well as estimating how they would use their time over the long term. As a result, some projects had to be delayed — this was a big step toward reversing their magical thinking that they could do everything at once. The Priority Action Plans led to negotiating realistic time allocated to these priorities for the next 6 months.

Projects. Leaders recognized the need to limit babble about operational issues during their meetings and to focus more on strategic thinking and steering. One project they undertook was to improve their meetings and decision-making. The group members all learned how to facilitate their meetings, manage the flow of the discussions, and make decisions that were understood by all group members.

Coaching. During individual coaching, members were encouraged to explore some dysfunctional behaviors and factors that prevented them from being more effective as leaders. The insights from those coaching sessions were shared with the large group in order to collectively wrestle with the issues and find resolutions.

The problems the leaders tackled were long standing; on numerous occasions in the past years, they tried to implement new ways of working but failed to sustain new behaviors. It is like in the old saying, "Everyone knew the way, but no one really walked it." Using the SEAM tools helped them become more disciplined. As a result, the leaders altered their priorities, freed themselves from unnecessary tasks, and found time and opportunities for more strategic work. Altogether, having the data about dysfunctions and hidden costs, the deliberate use of

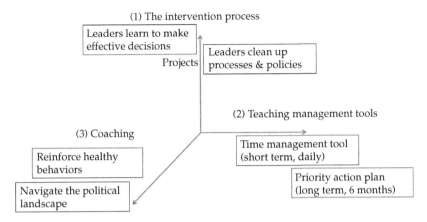

Figure 6.7.   A visual representation of socio-economic elements that addressed the problem of being overwhelmed. Similar approaches were undertaken to deal with every high-cost problem, identified during the diagnostic stage of the intervention.

management tools and regular coaching helped leaders to develop the new behaviors. The new behaviors were sustained for a longer time until they became habits. The leaders were able to model and help mid-level managers to do the same. The new way of working started cascading down throughout the organization.

Summary

The problems of magical thinking and failed initiatives are very common, yet they are not on the radar of many organizations. These problems trigger many other dysfunctions and lead to significant hidden costs. SEAM proved to be very effective in dealing with these and other problems by creating and supporting the healthy organizational system. The system is healthy when people and resources are aligned, and the talents and energy of people are used wisely. A healthy system is conducive to implementing sustainable initiatives that lead to organizational improvements and growth.

Chapter 7

SEAM Fosters a Culture of Transformative Learning

The systemic and deliberately paced intervention, as well as the focus on the socio-economics, makes the socio-economic approach to management (SEAM) the best organizational culture change approach. One of the factors is that with SEAM, people, through learning, change some of their deep beliefs and assumptions about management and the nature of work. This chapter provides the basic understanding of the concept of organizational culture, organizational learning and explains how SEAM has become a successful process for changing an organization's culture.

Organizational Culture

According to Edgar Schein, whose work focused on organizational culture and process consultation, organizational culture should be taken seriously, by which he meant not underestimating the impact the culture has on the overall effectiveness of the organization. Additionally, taking culture seriously includes having a good understanding of what constitutes culture.

What is culture? After a new group of individuals is formed, the group will develop norms and rules of behaviors about social interactions within the group, with other groups, and with the external environment. These norms become traditions and are reinforced by symbols and rituals.

The traditions are passed on to new members when they join the group. All members of the group are supposed to follow the group norms. The members who do not follow the norms are forced to accept the norms or are excluded from the group.

Over time, the norms are taken for granted by the group members and rarely if ever discussed in everyday interactions. These taken for granted assumptions become tacit knowledge and are the essence of the group culture. The group members may not remember or know the reasons behind some traditions or rules. Nevertheless, the group members follow the traditions and reject those who challenge them.

Culture is a learned response of a group to the external environment. Any social group will have its own unique culture, depending on which external challenges the group faces. Culture is a distinctive characteristic of a group. Schein compared the culture of a group to the personality of an individual.

There are many definitions of culture. The common themes in these definitions include the following:

- Culture is "shared" by a group of people.
- Culture is "distinctive" to a group (like a character or personality to an individual).
- Culture is "learned" by all members and "passed on" to new members in dynamic social interaction.
- Culture "guides" acceptable and unacceptable "behaviors" (thoughts, feelings, perceptions).
- Culture consists of explicit and "tacit assumptions" (conscious and unconscious).

Organizational culture. Organizational culture will have the same patterns of culture that any group has. This established way of functioning, whether good or bad, serves two important roles: it reduces cognitive and interpersonal uncertainty, and creates a feeling of predictable harmony for all members.

Schein's model of organizational culture is depicted by a pyramid with three levels — artifacts, espoused values, and underlying assumptions. On the top of the pyramid are "artifacts" that are visible and tangible organizational structures, processes, and behaviors. Offices, furniture, colors, dress code, mission statements, slogans, organizational rituals are some of the examples of artifacts. The artifacts can be easily seen by any observer who enters the organization.

The middle part of the pyramid contains the "espoused values" of the organizational culture. Espoused values reflect what the organization says it values and may pertain to customer service (e.g., quality, attitudes), internal environment (e.g., attitudes, trust, support, diversity), or relationship with external parties and communities (e.g., support, charity, loyalty). Espoused values are shared and widely expressed by the organization's members.

The third level, at the bottom of the pyramid, is where "underlying assumptions" reside. By assumptions, Schein meant the beliefs and values that shape people's behavior. Argyris used the term "governing beliefs" to describe underlying assumptions. It has been said that organizational culture is the way people behave when no one is watching. Behavior is shaped by people's underlying assumptions.

In a group, the shared assumptions are the core of the culture. These assumptions can be explicit or tacit, and conscious or unconscious. This third level of organizational culture contains unspoken rules, taboos, and undiscussable topics. So, even if some of the underlying assumptions are conscious, they usually are not discussed. If assumptions are unconscious, they cannot be identified or discussed. Both conscious and unconscious cultural assumptions shape people's understanding of what is good or bad and drive their behavior and interactions.

Often, there is a discrepancy between the espoused values and how people in the organization act.

Evaluating culture. Knowledge about organizational culture is useful when it comes to evaluating or changing culture. There are many companies that do organizational culture assessments, or even worse, culture surveys. Using Schein's model, it is clear that surveys and interviews can collect information only about artifacts and espoused values.

The assumptions that drive actual cultural behaviors are very difficult to assess. Some of the assumptions are undiscussable, and some are beyond the conscious awareness of people. Even people, who at first can understand the deepest level of organizational culture, over time become acclimatized to the underlying assumptions and stop seeing them.

People also stop seeing the discrepancy between their espoused values and their underlying assumptions. For example, an organization may profess that it believes in taking care of employees (espoused values) and at the same time behave in a way that hurts employees or their interests. Inability to see discrepancies between what is espoused and what is lived leads to the blindness that is associated with Argyris's organizational defensive routines (see Chapter 5).

Surveys and simple interviews with organizational members cannot accurately uncover the third level of underlying assumptions. It is simply impossible for people to talk about assumptions that are unconscious. To study the level of underlying assumptions of organizational culture, a different approach is needed. Ethnography is the methodology used to study cultures. Ethnography uses methods of observations and in-depth interviews of culture informants to collect data. Observations are especially helpful in identifying gaps between what people espouse and how they actually behave. Figure 7.1 shows where the research methods and elements of organizational culture overlap, leaving out some areas of organizational culture that cannot be assessed by any research.

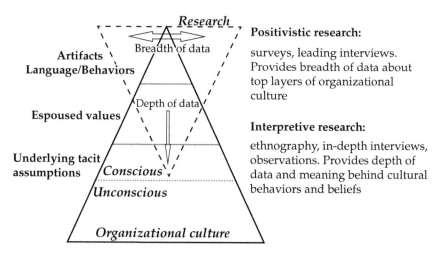

Figure 7.1.   Elements of organizational culture that can be assessed by different research methods. Unconscious parts of organizational culture are much more difficult to assess.

Changing culture. It is easier to make changes on the first two levels of organizational culture. To change the level of underlying assumptions is very difficult as they were originally formed in response to the external environment. Changing organizational visible artifacts or replacing espoused values will not in themselves change the organization's culture. Changing culture involves unlearning some old cultural behaviors and replacing them with new cultural behaviors. In order to unlearn some behaviors, challenging and changing some underlying assumptions are necessary. Schein warned that because culture is a learned thing, it will not change because someone announced it. Yet, the type of learning that is required for change will not come by training all employees. If learning does not involve change in the underlying assumptions at the deepest level of organizational culture, the organizational culture will remain the same. To change culture, a transformative learning of members is needed.

Culture Change Involves Transformative Learning

Two kinds of learning. There are two types of learning — informative and transformative. Informative learning allows people to learn more about the things that fit their mental models. Examples of informative learning would be language learning or professional training. Transformative learning is the process of changing mental models — changing one's set of underlying beliefs and assumptions. Other familiar terms used to describe change of mental model would be changing governing beliefs (Chris Argyris), paradigm shift (Thomas Kuhn), or changing a frame of reference. Transformative learning challenges some of the old worldviews and assumptions, with the result that some are changed. Examples of the results of transformative learning would be changing one's life style, adapting to a new culture, or choosing to do things that previously would be judged negatively.

Stages of transformative learning. Transformative learning happens in stages. To illustrate these stages, think of a person encountering a very different culture. In the first stage, "rejection," the person rejects any new knowledge that does not fit in his or her current mental model. Along with rejection, the person may judge, ridicule, or have other negative reactions and emotions. Whatever is different is wrong.

In the second stage, "understanding," the person gets used to the idea that there is another set of views, beliefs, and assumptions. While the person does not change his or her current mental model, he or she accepts that the other mental models exist. For example, traveling in a totally different cultural environment, a tourist may observe, and even admire, a different way of living, yet will follow his or her own cultural norms and behaviors.

In the third stage, "using," the person tries out new behaviors informed by a different mental model, either by choice, or because this is the only way to adapt to a new environment. For example, the person lives in a different culture for a longer time and finds some customs of this new culture acceptable and worth trying out. The person may try different foods, perform new activities, and have new cultural experiences but does not feel that they are something to embrace permanently.

On the fourth stage, "integration," the person forms a new mental model that incorporates the best elements of the old and different mental models and rejects elements of both that do not work. The new mental model informs the person's new behaviors. This is the stage when transformative learning is completed. In the cultural example, the person becomes bi-cultural. The person's new mental model becomes an amalgam of beliefs and assumptions from the old and different mental models that work in the new environment. Previous knowledge that does not work anymore in the new environment is rejected.

In Figure 7.2, the cylinder represents one's mental model and the arrows depict ideas that are taken in. The solid line arrow represents any new knowledge that fits one's current mental model, and the dashed line represents ideas from a different mental model.

The reader may see in Figure 7.2 that a person uses knowledge from a different mental model in the last two stages of transformative learning and wonder what the difference is between the two. The difference is that in Stage 3, the person's new behaviors are temporary, as the person still has the assumptions from the old mental model. In Stage 4, the underlying assumptions behind the behavior are changed. The person transformed. Mezirow, who wrote about transformative learning, indicated that Stage 4 is where "the habits of mind" change.

1. Rejection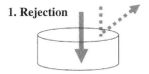

New knowledge (*dash line*) that does not fit in one's current mental model is rejected and judged. Only knowledge that fits (*solid line*) is accepted.

2. Understanding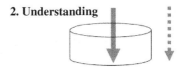

One understands that there are other mental models with different knowledge.

3. Using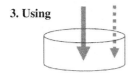

One tests new knowledge by trying to use it occasionally.

4. Integration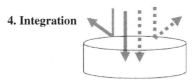

One sees the benefit of new knowledge and limitations of old knowledge; integrates knowledge from two mental models by taking and rejecting elements from both.

Figure 7.2.   The four stages of transformative learning.

To change organizational culture, people in an organization have to go through the fourth stage of transformative learning. This is the level at which the organizational culture change happens. The organization that requires people behave differently without changing the underlying assumptions informing employees' behaviors really does not change its culture. To change, people in an organization have to be able to explore safely their existing basic underlying assumptions. This is difficult work. Schein (2004) explained this difficulty well. He noted that

> Basic assumptions, like theories-in-use, tend to be *nonconfrontable* and *nondebatable*, and hence are extremely difficult to change. To learn something new in this realm requires people to resurrect, reexamine, and possibly change some of the more stable portions of their cognitive structure — a process that Argyris and others have called "double-loop learning" or "frame breaking" (Argyris *et al.*, 1985; Bartunek, 1984). Such learning is intrinsically difficult because the reexamination of basic assumptions temporarily destabilizes cognitive and interpersonal status quo, which releases huge amount of anxiety. (p. 31)

SEAM Through the Lens of Transformative Learning

SEAM helps people to go through transformative learning, and this is why it is successful in assisting organizational culture change. Two different models of transformative learning that complement each other are used to show how instrumental SEAM is in the organizational transformative learning.

The first model was posited by Mezirow (2000) who wrote that "Learning is understood as the process of using a prior interpretation to construe a new or revised interpretation of the meaning of one's experience as a guide to future action" (p. 5). Thus, learning is the process of taking what people know from the past, understanding this knowledge in a new way, and using this new knowledge to shape a new behavior in the future. This is different from learning a new language or a new theory. This type of learning is a challenge to people's previous beliefs and assumptions about what is true.

Mezirow also described transformative learning as objective and subjective. Objective reframing involves wrestling with the assumptions of others, as in task-oriented problem-solving processes such as action learning. Subjective reframing comes from self-reflection, wrestling with one's own assumptions. As Mezirow (2000) wrote, "Transformative learning, especially when it involves subjective reframing, is often an intensely threatening emotional experience in which we have to become aware of both the assumptions underlying our ideas and those supporting our emotional responses to the need to change" (p. 7). The emphasis on threat to the person parallels the caution of Schein.

Objective reframing might involve a group wrestling together to decide how to do something more effectively. An example of subjective reframing in an organization is Argyris's double-loop learning, in which the individual changes on the level of governing beliefs. In a SEAM intervention, both objective and subjective reframing occur. The line between subjective and objective reframing can be blurry. For instance, for a leadership group to change objectively, each of the group members may need to undergo subjective reframing.

SEAM Through the Lens of Mezirow's 10 Steps of Transformation

Mezirow outlined the usual process of transformation. This is a general outline, not a rigid set of steps through which one mechanically marches. Based on people's characteristics, their maturity and level of awareness, these steps can differ. However, the pattern will be somewhat the same — from a first encounter with a different phenomenon, through psychological and emotional works, to making the phenomenon part of one's mental model.

1. A disorienting dilemma
2. Self-examination with feelings of fear, anger, guilt, or shame
3. A critical assessment of assumptions
4. Recognition that one's discontent and the process of transformation are shared
5. Exploration of options for new roles, relationships, and actions
6. Planning a new course of action
7. Acquiring knowledge and skills for implementing one's plans
8. Provisional trying of new roles
9. Building competence and self-confidence in new roles and relationships
10. A reintegration into one's life on the basis of conditions dictated by one's new perspective (Mezirow, 2004, p. 22)

For many people, transformation through learning is somewhat accidental. A common source of transformation is foreign travel, in which the experience of a different culture causes people to re-examine their own cultural assumptions. Culture shock ensues, out of which the person chooses what practices to accept from the new culture and what to drop as a practice from the old culture.

Events happening in a SEAM intervention are not accidental. The SEAM process is designed to deliberately lead actors through transformative learning. The Mirror Effect and demonstration of hidden costs constitute a disorienting dilemma. The dilemma is reinforced by the

Expert Opinion, and for managers by the teaching about socio-economic theory and the management tools. Actors begin to recognize the flawed assumptions of the old mental model of management that prevent the organizations from being effective. This recognition does not happen quickly and easily; it involves a variety of feelings and emotions on the actors' part. Some actors may resist at first and some may be anxious or feel threatened. Over time, with support of the top leaders, actors begin to recognize the need to change and create a new management system, one that is more productive, more participative, more effective, and more joyous. Coaching can be helpful to assist actors in their transformational learning.

Actors begin to test new ways of managing. Better communication and cooperation begin to happen, and people's hope, that SEAM might work after all, grows. The projects are the immediate instances of planning a new course of action. The management tools reinforce realistic planning and reduce magical thinking about use of time. In the process of planning, actors are pressed to consider two tasks — (1) maintaining the work of the moment and (2) developing the human potential to grow the organization. For many organizations, this is a cultural turning point, in which the concern for developing human potential becomes as important as the completion of the daily maintenance tasks.

Mezirow's 10 steps of transformative learning are implicit in the SEAM process. While these steps are not neatly orchestrated into one specific order, these steps are very obvious through different phases of the SEAM intervention process (Table 7.1).

Support from leaders and the intervener-researchers reinforces the new habits of mind. It takes time for the transformation to become truly the new way to work. The deliberate timing and pace of the change process that is incorporated into a SEAM intervention allow actors enough time to go through the transformative learning. As the SEAM intervention settles into becoming the new way of working, the benefits of the transformation increase over time.

Table 7.1. Mezirow's 10 steps of transformative learning in the SEAM process.

Mezirow's 10 steps of transformation	SEAM activities and elements that reinforce steps of transformation
1. A disorienting dilemma	The diagnostic phase (Mirror Effect and Expert Opinion) results in a disorienting dilemma
2. Self-examination with feelings of fear, anger, guilt, or shame	Actors may have feelings of guilt or shame as they realize the number of dysfunctions in what they thought was an effective organization
3. A critical assessment of assumptions	Reflecting on the discrepancy between traditional model of management and SEAM; traditional and SEAM's accounting systems
4. Recognition that one's discontent and the process of transformation are shared	Begins in the Mirror Effect as actors realize that other actors share discomfort at the organizational dysfunctions
5. Exploration of options for new roles, relationships, and actions	Happens through involvement in projects and through coaching; organizational leaders model change and new behaviors
6. Planning a new course of action	Begins with the projects and the Internal/External Strategic Action Plan; continues with Priority Action Plans and Personally Negotiated Activity Contracts
7. Acquiring knowledge and skills for implementing one's plans	New learning opportunities for actors are reinforced by competency grids and provided through training
8. Provisional trying of new roles	As the SEAM intervention continues, managers and other actors test out new ways of behaving in the workplace
9. Building competence and self-confidence in new roles and relationships	Actors test new roles and skills, gaining competence and confidence over time
10. A reintegration into one's life based on conditions dictated by one's new perspective	Happens over time; at a personal level, the new model of management becomes comfortable; at the organizational level, change in culture

Four Conditions for Transformative Learning

Another way to look at transformative learning is through the framework of Daloz (2000). According to Daloz's model, four conditions are needed for people to engage in the difficult task of transformative learning.

The presence of *the Other*. The first condition is the presence of *the Other*. *The Other* is the person, or people, who carry different assumptions than oneself and so have different habits and behaviors. The presence of *the Other* pushes one to re-examine one's own basic assumptions. If *the Other* is not present, then there is no way to be exposed to a different mental model and ways of doing things, and no impetus to examine one's own assumptions.

Reflective discourse. The second condition needed for transformative *learning* is reflective discourse. Frequently discourse is intended to inform or convince people. Reflective discourse seeks common understanding and is inherently non-judgmental. Reflective discourse requires a level of emotional maturity and emotional intelligence. As one explores one's own values, placing them next to *the Other's* different values, the tendency is to start with the belief that one's own values are better. Reflective discourse means internal and external dialogue in which one examines differences, tries new concepts on, and sees if new things make sense.

As simple as that may sound, the process of reflective discourse can be unsettling. In SEAM, managers are faced with the premise that much of what they have learned is not effective and may indeed damage employees and productivity. It takes emotional maturity to accept the premise as worth examining. It is hard to accept what managers been taught and done for years may be flawed. It is harder to accept the premise that one's management style may have been hurtful. However, without such discourse, one can never gain enough distance from one's own closely held beliefs. Distancing oneself from one's own beliefs is needed to be open to learning.

Mentoring community. A mentoring community is the third condition for transformative learning. Since changing one's beliefs and values can be internally threatening, the process is easier when there is a group of people who share the transformational anxieties. The mentoring

Figure 7.3. Daloz's four conditions for transformative learning.

community is a group of people with whom one can have reflective discourse, during which one finds guidance and support. With the help of the mentoring community, one can safely explore differences and decide what beliefs and values from the old and new mental models to keep and what to discard.

The opportunity for committed action. Finally, transformative learning cannot be just cognitive, it needs to lead to actions in which one tests the new beliefs and behaviors. The fourth condition of transformative learning is having the opportunity for actions and being committed to change. If one is not behaving differently after trying to act, then there probably has not been real transformative learning. Figure 7.3 visually summarizes the four conditions for transformative learning.

SEAM Provides the Conditions for Transformative Learning

Learning about SEAM is a transformative learning experience for many managers. However, SEAM fosters the right environment for the transformative learning to occur. Using Daloz's model, it is easy to see how SEAM provides the conditions needed for actors' transformative learning. In turn, actors' transformation will lead to change of the organization's culture.

The presence of *the Other.* The current management practices are the result of managerial theories developed during the late industrial revolution, which in socio-economic theory are called the Taylorism, Fayolism, Weberism (TFW) virus (see Chapter 2). Following is a brief summary of the flawed assumptions of the TFW virus and the outcomes (last three points):

- The purpose of business is profit.
- People are disposable and are the first resource to be cut in the time of crisis.
- Leaders do all decision-making and fix problems.
- Leaders do not have structures to hear the voices of people lower in the hierarchy.
- Hyper-specialization is most effective.
- Employees must be obedient.
- Being a manager does not mean one knows how to manage.
- The price for manager's poor decisions is paid by employees lower in the hierarchy.
- Hidden costs are not measured.

When an organization commits to improvement, it is exposed to SEAM. In a way, SEAM is *the Other* and is embodied in the intervener-researchers. Starting with a different mental model and ending with some different practices, SEAM challenges the basic assumptions of traditional management and offers a new way of understanding management. Table 7.2 provides the major differences between the two mental models of management.

At first, the intervener-researchers are *the Other* as they introduce the organization to *the other* model of management. Later, as the intervention grows in an organization, the group of leaders becomes *the Other* for the rest of the organization.

Reflective discourse. Discussing new ideas happens in several ways. In learning about socio-economic theory and management tools, managers have a chance to talk through differences and concerns. In the Mirror Effect, actors see the amount of the dysfunctions and hidden costs, and they talk with each other and to intervener-researchers. Some may argue

Table 7.2.   Traditional and socio-economic models of management.

Traditional management	Socio-economic management
The mental model is rooted in ideas of industrial revolution, the TFW virus	The mental model is based on socio-economic theory
Focus on economic aspects of the organization	Focus on both human and economic aspects of the organization
Employees are capital to be used as long as they benefit the organization and then discarded	Developing human potential is the source to increasing organizational value
Traditional accounting does not measure hidden costs	Hidden costs are measured, averaging over $20,000 per employee per year
In organizational change, the focus is on structures and behaviors	In organizational change, the focus is on identifying and reducing dysfunctions, hidden costs
Employees should be obedient	All actors should negotiate when their needs are not met

and question whether the data are accurate. There is a chance that the Mirror Effect session may start a dialogue between actors, in which they wrestle and reconcile with the need to change. This is part of the value of waiting a month before holding the Expert Opinion — the time allows for reflective discourse. This dialogue may continue as the Expert Opinion, in which the intervener-researchers add their insights to the discussion.

Two things have happened at this point. Actors began a new kind of discourse throughout the organization, talking without fear about real problems. At the same time, quietly, the old assumptions began to be questioned and, without pressure, began to change. An example is the supervisor who discovered that she did not have to punish people every time they made a mistake. While this discovery may seem simple, it involved emotional wrestling that accompanied the cognitive challenge of a deeply held belief about supervision.

The mentoring community. Within the organization, a mentoring community forms. This starts with the SEAM intervener-researchers teaching, coaching, and modeling the organizational leaders. As the intervention cascades through the organization, the leaders become the mentoring community for each new part of the organization that is introduced with SEAM. During intervention, intervener-researchers train internal SEAM champions, whose role is to keep the process going. These trained internal champions become part of the mentoring community for every new unit involved in the intervention.

In France, ISEOR serves as the primary mentoring community for intervener-researchers. Conferences, teaching, publishing, and a variety of formal and informal meetings are the context for the mentoring. In the United States, the mentoring community for intervener-researchers is in the process of forming through efforts of interested individuals, schools, and the SEAM Institute. The SEAM Institute has organized annual US SEAM conferences since 2012. The purpose of the conferences is to provide a forum for gathering intervener-researchers across the United States in order to develop a comprehensive and knowledgeable mentoring community.

Opportunities for committed action. Within the organization, the opportunity for committed action begins with the projects. The Expert Opinion leads to direct actions, a series of projects designed to be inclusive and collaborative. Each project aims to reduce dysfunctions and hidden costs, and increase the opportunities to develop human potential. Usually, actors quickly volunteer to participate in the improvement of the silo or organization.

The projects are the means for actors to apply new knowledge and test new beliefs. For example, actors begin to negotiate with their supervisors about the use of time and priorities. Before SEAM, most actors believe that negotiation would never work. After SEAM, many actors are pleasantly surprised that negotiation works.

To conclude, whether the actors know about transformative learning theories or not, they will go through the learning process. The opportunity to learn is built in the SEAM intervention process. As a result, actors go through informative and transformative learning, subjective and objective reframing, and reflection and emotional work. All of the above contribute to the development of human potential.

Summary

Organizational culture is a set of shared assumptions, taken for granted, that help individuals respond to challenges. Organizational culture is composed of layers — visible artifacts, espoused values, and underlying tacit assumptions. Changing underlying assumptions, most of which are unconscious, is difficult, and this is the reason that organizational culture is hard and slow to change.

In order for organizational culture to change, the organization's members have to engage in the process of transformative learning. During transformative learning, a person's tacit assumptions and beliefs are challenged. Transformative learning happens in stages and requires certain conditions. Change of culture happens at the final stages of transformative learning.

The SEAM intervention process fosters and facilitates transformative learning of the members of an organization. Actors are engaged in learning and transformation, which results in a changed organizational culture.

Chapter 8

Why SEAM Is Not in the Mainstream

By this chapter, most readers have a pretty good idea of socio-economic approach to management (SEAM) as a different mental model for management and what constitutes an effective workplace. At the same time, some may ponder if SEAM is so good in making an organization effective, then why is SEAM not widely known and practiced in the US? There are several reasons that SEAM is not in the mainstream. This chapter provides a detailed explanation of the most significant reasons.

Language Issues

One reason for the lack of public awareness of SEAM in the US is that SEAM is a French creation. The original writing about SEAM was in French, teaching about SEAM was mostly in French and Spanish and most SEAM interventions were done in francophone countries. While the ISEOR team began its internationalization strategy in the1990s, it took some time to publish about SEAM in English. The *Journal of Organizational Change Management* had an issue devoted to SEAM in 2003. *Socio-Economic Intervention in Organizations, the Intervener-Researcher and SEAM Approach to Organizational Analysis*, edited by Anthony Buono and Henri Savall, was published in 2007. *Mastering*

Hidden Costs and Socio-Economic Performance by Henri Savall and Veronique Zardet was published in French in 1987 but was not released in English until 2008.

SEAM was taught at ISEOR and the University of Lyon in French (and Spanish at ISEOR), and it was not until 2008 that seminars in English and in French were offered by ISEOR.

The Separation of Theory and Practice

In France, despite its high reputation among some business people and corporate CEOs, the SEAM approach is not a mainstream approach to management. The reason lies in a division between the academia and practice in France. Academics are expected to stay in the academy and wrestle with conceptual stuff, and not to meddle in the field. For some French academics, the work of intervener-researchers is not acceptable because in their minds the academic work has been adulterated with practice, and so it is not academically pure. Consulting, in turn, is believed to be the domain of application; so business people see academics as people who do not know how things work in real life. Thus, in France, there is a built-in chasm between research and practice. The intervener-researcher concept is a direct challenge to the French mental model of academia, and the tension between many academics and ISEOR is still present. There is a similar division between scholars and practitioners in the US, but the gap is wider in France.

The Need for Leaders to Change

From an organization's leadership, SEAM requires not only the understanding of the socio-economic premises of SEAM but also living them. Most organizations or leaders are not able or willing to do so. For many leaders, it is easier to push the change down and tell others to change than to change themselves. SEAM theory requires interventions to start from the top. This way, the leaders are the first in the organization, who embrace change. Later, the leaders model changes when the intervention cascades down to other silos in the organization.

Ironically, SEAM meets the espoused beliefs of many managers and leaders. SEAM provides an analysis of hidden costs, creates an exchange of information among all parts of an organization, and increases employee morale, all of which are very desirable. Many managers say they need effective processes, good communications, and a positive organizational climate; yet the same managers, when faced with the need to change, find excuses to either maintain the *status quo*, or find a quick fix solution to a problem. Their desire to keep *status quo* is understandable. To embrace SEAM, the organization has to enter into a period of transformational change — change that involves changing one's beliefs and the actions produced by these beliefs. Any significant organizational change is transformational learning, which takes some time. The predominant American model is that change should be done quickly. Positive results tend to be short term. The model of speedy change and the lack of permanent results prevent significant transformative learning.

Unfamiliar Jargon and Terms

People who try to study SEAM are introduced to several new terms that look strange, such as *generic contingency, contradictory inter-subjectivity, cognitive inter-activity,* and *qualimetrics.* These terms are somewhat difficult to grasp at first, unless one uses an epistemological lens. Yet, even one who is familiar with epistemology might be somewhat confused. The reason for confusion is based in language. In the first part of the 21st century, scholars in the social sciences have not agreed upon a common vocabulary for ontology, epistemology, and methodology. Therefore, it is necessary to explain some philosophical and research concepts before defining the SEAM terms. These research concepts pertain to the social sciences, which is very appropriate when dealing with organizations. What follows is our definitions of these terms.

Ontology refers to one's belief about the nature of reality. The accepted research ontology of the first part of the 20th century was objectivism, the belief that reality is unchanging and can be accurately discovered if the right tools are used. A second ontology, social constructionism, shaped interpretive research. Social constructionism is the belief that human meaning is created by societies, and thus there is no true human meaning. Each society creates its own true understanding of human meaning.

Epistemology refers to how one knows what is true. In the first part of the 20th century, research in the social and natural sciences was based on the scientific methods, and was called *positivism, natural science*, and/or *empiricism*. Positivism was so entrenched that it was seen by many philosophers "as identical with philosophy of science itself. Its basic definitions and distinctions were regarded as self-evident, and anyone who questioned them was contemptuously ignored as simply not a philosopher of science" (Diesing, 1991, p. 3). The mindset among many researchers was that positivism was the only research that merited the title science. This mindset is still prevalent in some parts of Europe and the US.

Positivistic research. Positivism is based on the belief that a researcher can be neutral and does not have an impact on what is being studied. Thus, the researcher can manage bias so that it will not have an effect on the data collection and analysis. The object of a study can be dissected into parts, which enhances the process of receiving valid information about the research topic.

A definition of positivism from an American research text book is that positivism is "the epistemological doctrine that physical and social reality is independent of those who observe it, and that observation of this reality, if unbiased, constitutes scientific knowledge" (Gall, Gall, & Borg, 2007, p. 16). The goal of positivistic research is to predict or control in order to be able to improve the world in some way. The heart of positivistic research is to have or develop a theory and then to test some hypothesis that comes from the theory. The definition of positivism with the emphasis that "the observation of this reality, if unbiased, constitutes scientific knowledge" illustrates the belief that only positivistic studies are real science.

Interpretive research. A second epistemological approach is interpretive research, also known as qualitative research, in which the goal is to discover and understand the meaning of a text, culture, phenomenon, or case. Interpretive research has a different set of assumptions than positivism. Interpretive research is based on the belief that neutrality is impossible because the researcher will inevitably have some impact on the subjects of the study. Thus, a researcher's bias is inevitable in interpretive research. Recognition of bias needs to be included in the narrative of the description of the research, so that the reader can assess the extent to which the bias led the researcher to certain results and conclusions. In fact, a researcher's bias can be a strength, helping the researcher to understand the studied phenomenon.

Interpretive research also implies a holistic approach, which means that a researcher must always study a topic in context. Denzin and Lincoln (2000) wrote that qualitative research "involves an interpretive, naturalistic approach to the world. This means that qualitative researchers study things in their natural settings, attempting to make sense of, or to interpret, phenomena in terms of the meanings people bring to them" (p. 3). The goal of interpretive research is understanding. The value of understanding is parallel to the common maxim about history; if one does not understand history, one is doomed to repeat it. One does not study history to be able to have accurate prediction or control over the future, but the usefulness of history is nonetheless clear. Interpretive research allows findings to emerge from data, rather than being limited by theories that shape data collection and analysis. A researcher has to be open to the world being studied.

Post-positivism. There is another approach in the social sciences, which is called by some as post-positivism. This begins with the acceptance that social constructionism is a valid ontology of research into human meaning. The methods used are positivistic with an understanding that there are different human approaches to what is real, but through the positivistic methods one can still discover new and useful information that can help one predict and control what will happen in the future.

The readers who know something about *quantitative* and *qualitative* research might find the following information useful. Some authors use quantitative and qualitative research to describe epistemology, so for them quantitative research is synonymous with positivism and qualitative is synonymous with interpretive research. Some researchers use these terms to describe methodologies and/or methods. Because both positivistic and interpretive researchers use quantitative and qualitative data, we prefer to use "positivistic" and "interpretive" research to define epistemologies and "quantitative" and "qualitative" research to define methods of data collection and analysis.

Epistemology wars. In the second half of the 20th century in the US, the positivistic and interpretive research approaches clashed. Many positivistic researchers were adamant that only positivistic research produced real science. In the social sciences, many researchers rejected positivism as a legitimate epistemology for social science research, a clash that has been called the "Epistemology Wars." Today, in the US, social scientists in general are willing to accept that both positivistic and interpretive researches have value.

In many European countries, and in some fields in the US, such as management and medicine, there is still a common attitude that positivistic research is more legitimate than interpretive research. Frequently, in France, there has been academic resistance to any research that did not look positivistic, especially when it came to management research. Therefore, the fact that the ISEOR researchers were developing a new approach to research that started with qualitative methods, by collecting information about human perceptions through interviews, had to generate some resistance from the French positivistic academics.

This French insistence on positivism as the only epistemology that leads to real science is the context for the development of socio-economic theory. Savall had the problem of convincing the French academy that his approach to research, in which elements of positivism, interpretivism, objectivism, and social constructionism are all used, is valid science. He developed the SEAM language that would reflect the scientific nature of the approach.

The Scientific Side of SEAM

In addition to being an organizational change intervention, SEAM involves complex theory-building research. This research is done in the post-positivistic epistemology within a social constructionist ontology, using both qualitative and quantitative methods of data collection and analysis (using the SEAM language, *qualimetrics*). The three terms below reflect the scientific, or scholarly, nature of SEAM.

Contradictory inter-subjectivity. The first term pertains to the diagnostic phase of a change intervention in organizations by intervener-researchers. The intervention itself has elements of interpretive and positivistic research. When intervener-researchers collect data, they are using a social constructionist lens in which the truth is socially constructed. The intervener-researchers use interpretive methods for data collection and analysis. Data are gathered through interviews, analyzed for themes, and presented back to the participants. There is no pretense that the intervener-researchers will find the exact truth, and discrepancies between participants are ignored, since each person brings his or her own truth. This is *contradictory inter-subjectivity*, which refers to the fact that actors perceive truth differently, and whatever the actors perceive is true according to their beliefs and perceptions. The actors interact and share their subjective perception with others, some of these perceptions may be contradictory.

Contradictory inter-subjectivity is the "technique for creating consensus based on the subjective perceptions of different actors, in order to create more 'objective' grounds for working together" (Buono & Savall, 2007, p. 423). This concept is a response to the belief that there is objective truth that can be discovered, which is not possible in the realm of human meaning and perception. Contradictory inter-subjectivity is similar to the ontological tenet in social constructionism in that the human meaning is socially constructed and therefore there can be more than one socially constructed reality.

Cognitive inter-activity. The second term pertains to the simultaneous change in the organizations during and after the collection of research data. There is no pretense: intervener-researchers change the organization and at the same time are changed by the organization. In France, this is close to heresy. Real academics do not consult, and consultants are not academics. Savall's intervener-researcher model challenged a basic assumption of many in the French academy. The concept *of cognitive inter-activity* recognizes the interpretive belief that bias and influence are normal in social science research.

There is a nuance here. The collection of quotes as the first step of the SEAM intervention is an interpretive process. The Mirror Effect is a presentation of the meaning actors see in their workplace. The Expert Opinion adds the intervener-researchers' observation of what they think are the underlying causes of the dysfunctions, i.e., their interpretation of meaning.

Cognitive inter-activity is the "interactive process (between intervener-researchers and company actors) of knowledge production through successive feedback loops with the steadfast goals of increasing the value of significant information processed by scientific work" (Buono & Savall, 2007, p. 422). Through the intervention, both intervener-researchers and actors learn from each other. This concept differs from the "Pure science" concept where the research does not affect the subject of the research with scientific conclusions until the "experiment" is over. The positivistic assumption is that because reality is objective, one can study reality without changing it. Cognitive inter-activity is equivalent to the interpretive epistemological tenet that research in social science always affects the people being studied and those who study them.

Generic contingency. During the change intervention, the intervener-researchers classify the dysfunctions, sorting them into categories that are then added to the ISEOR database. The data are used to understand larger trends across organizations, i.e., to develop theory. The development of theory about socio-economic interventions in organizations is reflected in in the term *generic contingency*. Theory building is a valid part of both positivistic and interpretive research. In this instance, the theory is refined through the analysis of the SEAM database. SEAM represents perhaps the best example of organizational change research influencing theory, which then shapes how organizational change agents do their work. The cycle is constant, has been at work for over 40 years, and is very effective. In SEAM, the scholar–practitioner divide has been overcome.

Generic contingency is the "epistemological principle introduced in the socio-economic theory that, while recognizing the operational specificities of organizations, postulates the existence of invariants that constitute generic rules embodying core knowledge that possesses a degree of stability and 'universality'" (Buono & Savall, 2007, p. 425).

The SEAM research does not match the mental model of research that some management researchers demand. There is no hypothesis testing, no sample is drawn randomly from a larger population, and no inferential statistical analysis and generalization are applied to the larger population. How can the research be valid in a positivistic sense? Such research is valid only if conducted within the positivistic case study methodology.

The positivistic approach to science held that generalizable knowledge is only produced by experimentation, which implies that none of the works of ISEOR is scientific nor is it generalizable. Generic contingency is similar to the approach used in the positivistic case study, described by Robert Yin, in which a theory is created and then tested in case studies. Replication (getting the same results in many case studies) leads to high validity of the case study theory, which is then generalizable to organizations.

Positivistic case study research. In the US, Robert Yin began writing about positivistic case studies in the 1980s. Case studies are useful for examining "a contemporary phenomenon in depth and within its real-life context, especially when the boundaries between phenomenon and context are not easily evident" (Yin, 2007, p. 18). Most case studies are interpretive in nature, and a researcher examines a case in order to understand a phenomenon in its context. Yin had a different case study design. According to Yin (2009), case studies benefit "from the prior development of theoretical propositions to guide data collection and analysis" (p. 19), and "for case studies, theory development as part of the design phase is essential" (p. 35). Although Yin did not define his approach to case studies in epistemological terms, he described a positivistic research approach that uses the collection and analysis of qualitative and quantitative data to reach conclusions about the validity of a theory.

The value of the positivistic case study is the ability to develop and test a theory to see whether it is supported. One case study cannot prove that a theory is valid, thus study replications are needed. In traditional positivistic studies, a researcher generalizes by having a sample of a population, and then through inferential statistics applies the findings to the larger population. However, in complex and changing situations, like human organizations, it may be impossible to create samples that can be generalized to a larger population. The organizations in their unique contexts are too complex. Therefore, Yin's suggestion to avoid statistical generalization and instead use analytical generalization makes great sense. Essentially, analytic generalization means having a theory, then testing it through multiple case studies, and lastly seeing if the theory is supported. At some point, through replication, one can claim that the theory seems to be valid. This is what happens in ISEOR. Each consulting case can be viewed as the opportunity to test the theory, developed from analyzing the previous cases. Figure 8.1 illustrates how practice informs research, which in turn helps to build theory, which can be applied to practice, and the cycle starts again.

During the intervention stage, SEAM relies heavily on interpretative approach, using qualitative, quantitative, and financial data. At the macro level, SEAM research lies within the social constructionist ontology and is legitimate positivistic research about management science. Collecting data across organizations for over 40 years allowed the ISEOR researchers to find commonalities among organizations and as a result, to predict what is likely to be present in the next organizations. Prediction and control (improving the organization) are characteristics of good positivistic research. So, every time the researchers go into a new organization they may predict the nature and number of certain variables, and see whether the actual intervention yielded their

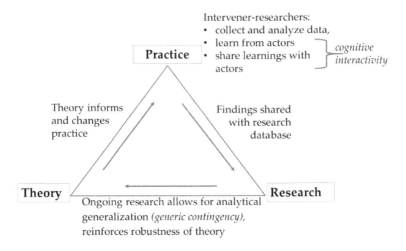

Figure 8.1.   The inter-relationship of practice, research, and theory in SEAM.

prediction. They also may find new unique elements to the organization. In the SEAM language, this is called *generic contingency*, which is the principle that allows for the uniqueness of each organization, and "postulates the existence of invariants that constitute generic invariants" (Savall, 2010, p. 2). It is obvious that generic contingency and analytic generalization are parallel concepts.

The use of the ISEOR jargon was justified by the need to establish the scientific nature of socio-economic research and introduce and raise the value of qualitative data in research. ISEOR's research stems from the ontology of social constructionism and uses post-positivistic epistemology. ISEOR, without naming it, uses a positivistic case study methodology, which works well in unique, complex, and changing situations such as human organizations. This methodology calls for testing theory through multiple case studies, or replications, to see whether the theory is supported. Using this methodology, a researcher cannot generalize findings to a larger population like in other positivistic methodologies. However, it is possible to apply research findings to the theory, in other words to provide an analytical generalization. At some point, through

Table 8.1.   Comparison of French and US terms.

French terms	Similar terms used in social sciences in the US	Meaning behind the term
Contradictory inter-subjectivity	Social constructionism	Different actors have different subjective perceptions of what is true.
Cognitive inter-activity	Researcher's bias in interpretive research	The intervener researchers cannot be a neutral observer.
Generic contingency	Analytical generalization	Testing theory through multiple case studies is a valid research methodology.
Qualimetrics	Mixed methods	Integration of qualitative and quantitative data to understand the complexity of phenomena.

replications, researchers can make a claim that the theory seems to be valid. Each SEAM intervention can be viewed as an opportunity to test the original theory, developed from analyzing the previous cases. Many scholars are not familiar with positivistic case study methodology and as a result, the validity and strength of the SEAM research might be discounted.

Summary

There are several reasons that SEAM is not known in the US. Although SEAM began in France in 1973, publications in English about SEAM only began in 2003. There is a chasm between academicians and practitioners in France that led to lack of appreciation of the scholar–practitioner nature of SEAM. In the US, the chasm is not quite as wide as in France, but this probably has had an effect on the acceptance of SEAM.

SEAM was developed during a time of changes in understanding about ontology and epistemology in social science research. Savall coined his own terms for concepts that were later described differently in the US. As a result, for an American reader, the socio-economic theory may have too much jargon.

Finally, SEAM only works when leaders are willing to change. Change is hard, and it takes courage to embrace SEAM. Moreover, SEAM takes time and it is not a quick fix that many organizations want.

Chapter 9

The Real Key to SEAM's Effectiveness

The socio-economic approach to management (SEAM) has a high level of effectiveness. Usually, organizations that invest in a SEAM intervention find that their financial investment in SEAM is returned within a year, and often within 3 months. Effectiveness is achieved through change intervention, teaching, and coaching based on socio-economic theory. This is at least what SEAM practitioners would say. What wouldn't they say? What are SEAM's "Non Dit" (in French for "what was not said")? This last chapter provides an insight into things that SEAM practitioners do not advertise, but perhaps these non-advertised elements make SEAM humane so effective.

The Elements of SEAM That Are Common in Consulting

In SEAM, the intervention is designed for the whole organization, weaving together elements of action research, training in management tools, and work on political and strategic tasks. Coaching leaders and facilitating group work support the whole system intervention. When one looks closely at these SEAM activities, it is obvious that none of them is that unique.

Many consultants intervene in organizations by collecting data, feeding it back to clients, and working with them to improve the organization. Many consultants teach how to manage, coach, and facilitate. The SEAM is whole system intervention, which involves leadership and cascades down through organizational silos. There are other whole system change processes, such as appreciative inquiry and large-scale change methodologies.

One might argue that SEAM has a disciplined discovery of hidden costs. However, there are consultants who are aware of hidden costs, and some who provide some approximation of hidden costs, although not with the level of research that one finds in SEAM. For instance, Swanson and Holton (1999) described a process in which consultants identified a problem, interviewed leaders to assess the extent of the problem, and then calculated a cost for the problem. Many consultants know how to calculate the costs of absenteeism, occupational injuries and diseases, staff turnover, poor quality, and rework. Yet, when identifying a problem and its hidden costs is the only element of any intervention, this element alone does not create lasting and positive change.

In terms of management tools, many other consultants help employees to examine their use of time, explore whether employees have the required competencies, and help with strategic planning. SEAM helps leaders make the political and strategic decisions to implement organizational change. This too is not exceptional. Analyzing political and strategic decisions is a common element in management consulting.

What makes SEAM unique is the combination of all tangible elements, described above, in one systemic intervention, which are supported by intangible SEAM core beliefs. The heart of SEAM is ethical, humane, and spiritual.

Ethics of SEAM

One ethical issue for SEAM is based on the theoretical premise that traditional accounting does not include all factors that lead to profit and loss in organizations; thus, traditional accounting yields inaccurate results. SEAM identifies these missing data as hidden costs, and then corrects the accounting problem by adding hidden costs to the organizational accounting system. SEAM also challenges the accuracy of traditional accounting that leaves out some of the human elements that shape organizational profit and loss.

The ethics of accounting. One ethical issue is how to respond to misleading and inaccurate accounting. By the tenets of the socio-economic theory, the decision-making processes used in most organizations are based on flawed and inadequate accounting. The ISEOR approach has quietly demonstrated the legitimacy of the socio-economic validity of SEAM. Since it is hard for many people to believe that one of the fundamental aspects of management is inadequate, it may take a long time before organizations accept that standard accounting is incomplete. It is always easier to dismiss the challenge than to do the work. The work in this case would be for organizations either to disprove the socio-economic approach to accounting, or to change their accounting practice.

There are two obvious ethical responses to the practice of flawed accounting. One is to quietly demonstrate that the SEAM practice is valid but traditional accounting is not. The other is to be more prophetic, publicly naming flawed accounting as inadequate and challenging its use. To date, champions of SEAM have chosen the route of quiet demonstration. Savall believes it is possible to change people's belief system through practice. Challenging people's beliefs directly can create vehement resistance. By using the SEAM process, people will experience a different way to work, and then will change their values and beliefs.

The ethics of developing human potential. The flawed accounting leads to another ethical issue. Most organizations do not recognize the value of human potential in measuring actual and potential profit and loss. The value of employees is measured by their salaries, not by their inputs in the organization's profit. This practice comes from Marxist and then neoclassical economics, in which the calculation of value is a function of two factors, capital and labor. Neither of these economic approaches considers the human potential, which is greater than hours of work, as it involves creativity, creation, idea generation, and other human contributions that refuse to be measured by hours. And because the human potential is not considered, and subsequently not developed, it turns into hidden cost.

Contemporary business and management theory treats people as a disposable commodity. The very term "human capital" reflects the belief that employees are a commodity. The idea of human capital leads to two ethical implications. The first implication is that when there is an economic crisis, the quickest solution is to reduce resources or diminish the workforce. Reduction of resources is done by firing people, which is masked by euphemisms such as "laying off," "down-sizing," or most cynical of all, "right-sizing." People, who did not make the choices that led to poor organizational performance, are fired, but the leaders who made poor decisions and failed to manage well, stay. People in power tend to keep their power, regardless of issues of ethics or justice.

The ethics of wealth. The Taylorism, Fayolism, Weberism (TFW) virus includes a belief that people at the top of the organization deserve to be treated differently from others. In the early 2000s, the leaders of the banking industry made choices that brought on a national financial crisis, which led to hundreds of thousands of people losing their homes, even while many banking leaders received multi-million-dollar bonuses.

Along with leaders escaping the responsibility for their poor decision-making, greed has shaped the way leaders are compensated compared with the average employee. *New York Times*'s Editorial writer Bob Herbert wrote

> Income and wealth inequality in the U.S. have reached stages that would make the third world blush. As the Economic Policy Institute has reported, the richest 10 percent of Americans received an unconscionable 100 percent of the average income growth in the years 2000 to 2007, the most recent extended period of economic expansion.
>
> Americans behave as if this is somehow normal or acceptable. It shouldn't be, and didn't used to be. Through much of the post-World War II era, income distribution was far more equitable, with the top 10 percent of families accounting for just a third of average income growth, and the bottom 90 percent receiving two-thirds. That seems like ancient history now. (March 25, 2011)

Such distribution of wealth is possible only if human beings and human potential are not highly valued, but rather are treated as resources to serve those in power. If the purpose of business is only to earn money, and by corollary, the purpose of managing is to earn money for self and business, then societies will never grow and develop.

The Periodically Negotiated Activity Contract is based on the belief that profits should be shared equitably. Socio-economic theory does not try to make all incomes equal, but seeks a less lop-sided sharing among the people who do the work. This approach is in line with Bernácer's argument that unearned income hurts the economy and ought to be abolished.

The purpose of business. SEAM recognizes the value of human beings in business and offers a different premise about the purpose of business. The purpose of business is to generate a profit, serve the persons who work in the organizations, and contribute to the maintenance of a healthy society. In the case on nonprofit organizations, instead of generating profit, the task becomes serving a portion of society. In the socio-economic theory, it is ethically unacceptable for an organization to solely seek monetary gain and to harm employees or society by means of earning its profit.

Moreover, every organization exists in a city, nation, planet. Part of the ethical requirement of the organization is to contribute to the common good in the community. This is at the heart of Socially Responsible Capitalism based on the thought of Bernácer and Perroux and articulated by Savall and his colleagues. For an American, Socially Responsible Capitalism might seem very French, very socialist. It is worth pointing out that the values are based in the Judeo-Christian tradition, which leads to the spiritual aspects of SEAM.

The Spirituality of SEAM

Spirituality involves a sense of connection between the human person and something larger than the person. Spirituality involves the search for meaning in life, and is a universal part of being human. Theology is the study of the divine. In Western society, Christian theology shaped beliefs about spirituality, faith, and religion for nearly two millennia.

Role of theology. In Europe, prior to the scientific revolution, theology was positioned as the queen of the sciences. This meant that other sciences were given a theological context. Simply put, all creations were from the deity, and were sacred because these were the deity's gifts. The lesser sciences, such as physics, astronomy, or biology existed to help humans understand and be stewards of creation. This stewardship included caring for nature and human beings. In the years since the scientific revolution, theology was separated from the natural and social sciences and the theological role of stewardship for science has been lost.

Once, Christian theology provided the moral and ethical context for science in Western culture. One can argue that the Church overstepped its role in resisting scientific discoveries, as in the case of Galileo, and so the Church lost its right to gauge the merit of the findings of science. Spiritual thought was separated from science, as if the two had nothing to do with each other. While this argument about the inability of the Church to assess the truth of scientific findings has merit, the spiritual context in which researchers do science is missing. Implicit in SEAM is a spiritual context.

The theological context. At the heart of the Biblical message is that human beings are important, not because of their achievements, but simply because they are. In the language and imagery of Christian baptism, all are named as brothers and sisters in Christ. Thus, the proper relationship with one's fellow human beings is a relationship of love, as in brotherly or sisterly love. People may dislike and disagree with other fellow human beings, or object to their actions. But the unavoidable command of the Gospels is to love all people. No matter how much people try to avoid it, this is the command: "Love one another as I have loved you" (John 13:34). This applies to work life as well as the rest of life.

Pope John XXIII (1963) wrote in *Pacem in Terris*, concerning the integration of faith and action:

> In traditionally Christian States at the present time, civil institutions evince a high degree of scientific and technical progress and possess abundant machinery for the attainment of every kind of objective. And yet it must be owned that these institutions are often but slightly affected by Christian motives and a Christian spirit. One may well ask the reason for this, since the men who have largely contributed — and who are still contributing — to the creation of these institutions are men who are professed Christians, and who live their lives, at least in part, in accordance with the precepts of the gospels. In Our opinion the explanation lies

in a certain cleavage between faith and practice. Their inner, spiritual unity must be restored, so that faith may be the light and love the motivating force of all their actions. (pp. 151–152)

The call for the restoration of a holistic understanding of spirituality challenges the premise that the purpose of business is solely to make money. The fact that spiritual claims are kept separate from business does not mean the claims are not valid. If an employee as human capital is used or disposed when not needed, then the management behavior is immoral.

Human beings are intelligent and creative. When their needs are not met, human beings become disobedient and look for ways to meet those needs. When the person's needs are met, and abilities are respected and developed, the person becomes a different kind of employee than the one who is disengaged from work. Through the development of the person's potential, both the person and the organization develop. Here is where spirituality and business meet. Developing the whole person leads to more effective organizations.

Love as the Core "Non Dit" Belief of SEAM

The core belief that shapes the SEAM change process is that all actors need to be accepted unconditionally without judgment and blame. In other words, the guiding principle about how all actors ought to be treated is love.

Definitions of love. In English, the word love has several meanings. C. S. Lewis (1971) identified four different kinds of love: affection, friendship, romantic, and unconditional. Affection is the fondness held for others, such as with family and co-workers. Friendship is the strong and loving relationship between friends. Romance, or "eros," is love between lovers. Unconditional love, "agape" in Greek, or "caritas" in Latin, is what Lewis sees as the greatest of all loves. In other words, unconditional love means accepting people as they are, without judgment and without insistence that they change. Caring and respect are aspects of the unqualified acceptance, or unconditional love.

SEAM definition of love. A SEAM definition of love can be described as "an absolute respect of a person, or of people in general."

This definition of love is identical to the Greek "agape" and Latin "caritas." Accepting people unconditionally does not imply that one also accepts all their behaviors. It is possible to challenge a behavior without judging or rejecting the person. Love and sustainable human relations are demanding rather than complacent. So, love means accepting and not judging the person, and being very clear about actions that are and are not acceptable. This is tough love, the love that recognizes that some behavior is not professional, not brave, not supportive of interests of the team, and thus is not acceptable. Love can be seen in SEAM's practice of not blaming people, and focusing on the organization system's problems.

The damage done by the TFW virus. Many organizations espouse the value of treating each person with respect. And yet such respect is rarely found in organizations. The question is why? The answer lies within a system of destructive beliefs about management, the TFW virus. Most organizations in the Western society are infected by it, and the virus is the antithesis of love. A workplace in which the TFW virus has taken hold can be recognized by disrespectful, fear-inducing, humiliating behaviors on the part of managers. Here is an example of how deeply the TFW virus is ingrained into the mental model of current management.

Many are familiar with the controversial practice "rank and yank" attributed to the former General Electric Company CEO Jack Welch. According to this practice, managers should assess their employees every year and divide them into three categories: the top 20%, the middle 70%, and the bottom 10%. The top 20% should be praised and financially rewarded. The middle 70% should be motivated and supported to get into the top 20. And the rest 10% have to go. As a result, the forced ranking practice not only undermines team work, but also reduces the organizational effectiveness in the long term. This practice encourages employees to engage in destructive and game-playing behaviors, and corrupts their souls.

The scandal at Wells Fargo Bank in 2016–2017 is another example of the destructive outcome of the TFW virus. Employees were driven by fear to get customers to do more business. They secretly signed millions of customers up for services without the customers' knowledge. As a result, customers were hurt. Some customers had their car repossessed when this should not have happened. Other customers received poor credit reports

that hurt their ability to borrow money. In the American retributive crimi-
nal justice system, the issue is the bankers broke the law, and so should be
punished. From a holistic and spiritual viewpoint, the issue is relationship.
The bankers behaved in a manner that was unloving, and in doing so they
damaged their customers, their organization, and their community. The
bankers infected by the TFW virus were damaged too. They were driven
by their fear to act unethically and unlovingly to get more money for the
company. Profit was valued more than relationships, more than love.

People have the need to be creative and to have meaningful work, the
need to be valued as a person, heard and loved, or the need to have time
for self and family. These are spiritual needs. When a person is put into a
job that is mind-numbingly boring, or when the person is micromanaged
or threatened, damage is done to the human spirit and the human potential
is thwarted. An organization that does not meet actors' needs of developing potential, either deliberately or by neglect, is an unhealthy and unloving workplace that is destructive of actors' soul and spirit.

Love in the workplace. A primary goal of SEAM is to combat the
TFW virus, to inoculate the organization so that it rejects the virus and
becomes healthy. Love, "caritas," is the antidote to the TFW virus. SEAM
reduces unloving behavior so that all actors can thrive, and as a result the
organization can become more productive. An intervener-researcher could
do all the functions outlined in the SEAM trihedron, but if these were
done without love, the result would be different.

What does a loving workplace look like? Love at the workplace
means respecting the person as he or she is, and developing the person's
potential to the extent possible. To really respect an actor, leaders have to
invest time and effort in listening, trying to understand the other's point of
view and to contribute to the development of the person's potential.
However, it is easier to tell people what to do and dismiss those who are
wounded or need care, than to show love and respect. This is why the virus
lives in today's organizations, and decades of management consulting
have not made much progress in combating the virus.

SEAM is based on the premise that SEAM intervener-researchers,
and all actors in an organization, have the duty and the moral obligation
to help people grow closer to reaching their human potential. This duty to
help people grow applies even if people are not aware of their current lack

of growth because of the poor management system in which they live. The SEAM assumption is that most people would choose to grow and achieve, and if this is not the case, then the lack of ambition is most likely the result of educational and management practices that have wounded the actor. If actors have been wounded, what is the loving response? First is to recognize that the actor is wounded and in need of healing, to accept the actor as a human being, and then to provide help or the means for growth if the actor chooses to develop.

For instance, when an employee is not motivated by work, is it the fault of the employee to have accepted a job that either is not motivating or no longer motivating? Or is it the fault of the organization for hiring someone for work that is not interesting to the person? Looking for who is at fault implies blaming.

In SEAM, the question of "whose fault" is not even relevant. SEAM's view is that the person is not fitted to the particular job, and thus something needs to be done. Assessment of the cause of lack of motivation is necessary before any solution is applied. If the problem is lack of training, then training is needed. If the problem is caused by mental health issues, then medical care is needed. If the problem is that the actor is poorly supervised, then the actor's supervisor needs assistance. The point is to respect the needs of the individual, and work to meet these needs, as well as to meet the needs of the organization.

At the same time, it is important to note that respecting and nurturing employees do not mean putting up with anything the employees would do. When an employee is not performing well, the task of the manager is to understand the cause and provide assistance so that the employee can succeed.

The place of love in consulting. Love is not a topic that arises often in management consulting. Consultants and clients are focused on efficiency, effectiveness, and profit. Love is considered a soft concept, and probably is deemed irrelevant in the consulting process and in business itself. Moreover, many business people may judge and dismiss consultants who talk about love in the workplace.

Nonetheless, the SEAM intervener-researchers must begin with modeling love for the client organization. The intervener-researcher's love of the client organization is part of the SEAM philosophy, and a significant factor in their successful results. Indeed, the intervener-researcher's love for the actors allows actors to accept the harsh information about organizational dysfunctions and hidden costs. In addition, the modeling of unconditional acceptance by the researcher-interveners may help leaders to develop new relationships with the other actors in the organization.

The SEAM approach to organizational change is shaped by a profound belief in the value of every person, and as such is implicitly and deeply in harmony with spiritual teachings. Developing organizational capacity without harming the actors is a rare and courageous approach to change. Many change agents might say they do this, but the question is whether their espoused beliefs match their practice. In SEAM, love is "non dit," yet present in the work of the intervener-researcher in the intervention, and in the behaviors of all actors in the intervention progresses. SEAM is based on the practice of accepting all people in the organization and helping them develop.

Changing organizations with love. The question for the intervener-researcher is how to change the values and practices of the leaders and all actors, in a manner that leads to positive and sustainable change. This is a difficult task because leaders tend to resent being told that their approach to management is flawed. Employees, in turn, may be afraid of being fired if they expose their own failings, thus they may not be ready to be open to share. Often, actors assume that if they challenge organizational authorities, then they will be retaliated. Additionally, many actors have been part of some change work, pushed on them, or involved in change without much positive results. Thus, often, actors are skeptical of and resistant to change. How does SEAM overcome skepticism and resistance?

Rather than verbally promote beliefs and values, SEAM intervener-researchers model the behaviors that manifest love. A core value is that all actors are important, not because they are effective, but because they are people. The right way to respond to people is with love. When people are accepted without qualification, with respect and care, they feel the presence of love. It is the repeated actions that convince actors that they are loved, much more than words. In SEAM, the objective is not to make pronouncements about love. The objective is to demonstrate by actions that all actors are respected, accepted, and treated as human beings.

By treating all actors with respect and care, the intervener-researchers overcome much resistance. People are more willing to hear the negative aspects of their behavior if they know the person offers feedback without judgment, with a positive intention, and not out of any sense of superiority. In other words, when actors feel that the intervener-researchers mirror to them what is not working well, in a spirit of love, without judgment, the actors are more willing to listen.

Savall likes to say that all human beings are intelligent. All actors can tell the difference between being loved, and being treated like a disposable tool whose purpose is making a profit for someone else. Actors can recognize love in the actions of intervener-researchers. Encouraging actors' growth and development feels like love. Sometimes, loving may involve letting people live their life and leave, if they choose not to work in accordance with the rest of the organization. SEAM is based on the development of human potential and development through love but not through fear. Intervener-researchers bring love into the consulting process and this is one of the reasons why SEAM is effective.

Summary

SEAM interventions include many elements that are used in other consulting approaches. At the same time, SEAM is different. There is something in the socio-economic theory and SEAM practice that makes SEAM interventions to be highly successful in creating effective and sustainable organizational change.

Socio-economic theory challenges the widespread belief that the purpose of business is profit. Instead, the socio-economic theory argues that it is equally important for organizations to serve the communities in which the organizations are located. Developing human potential is an important ethical practice that supports the spiritual health of individuals and the growth of the organization.

Spirituality is concerned with the whole person, and the whole organization and community. SEAM rejects the separation of spiritual concerns from business concerns. Absence of spirituality leads to heartless organizations. The SEAM approach includes a deep respect for all individuals and accepts people as they are. This loving, non-judging approach is a key factor in the success of SEAM interventions.

Afterword

Most organizations are not reaching their potential. As a result, some organizations struggle or die. Competition is strong in the world of organizations. For-profit organizations compete for profit. Non-profit organizations compete for the funds to provide services. To succeed in competition for an organization means to have a future.

For an organization in the future to thrive, having the best technology, equipment, and ideas is not enough. To succeed in the future, an organization needs skilled employees with the knowledge and competence to manage complex tasks and employees with sufficient emotional intelligence and organizational awareness. Such employees will be in great demand and organizations will compete for them.

Pay is not enough to keep many employees with an organization. It has been said that the main reason many people leave a job is their supervisor. To the extent to which this is true, for organizations to be competitive, they must develop a management system that does not foster supervisors who drive away employees.

Yet, when it comes to traditional management, some of the management assumptions are flawed. The mental model of management is infected by the Taylorism, Fayolism, Weberism (TFW) virus. The current mental model of management leads to the evaporation of employee energy, crushing their spirit. This is the reason of low employee engagement in the workplace. The socio-economic approach to management focuses on changing the way people manage. SEAM helps those who have been infected by the TFW virus to learn how to manage in a way that raises the spirit of workers. The change involves two parts: refocusing on where managers spend their time and effort, particularly on steering, and how managers treat others in the workplace.

One of the ways to increase organizational effectiveness is to increase cohesion in the workforce and create a collaborative and participative workplace. When actors work together, highly engaged in their work, they create energy. Many managers do not know how to create the participative workplace. Additionally, many organizations have cultures that are not conducive to participative management. The SEAM intervention is designed to assist in the development of a participative workplace with effective managers.

At first glance, SEAM appears to have a deficit-based focus, finding and reducing dysfunctions and hidden costs. However, the reduction of dysfunctions and hidden costs are the means to creating the capacity for organizations to find and embrace new opportunities. Part of the capacity building is achieved by reducing the time and money wasted by dysfunctions, and releasing energy for development and creation of potential.

There are ethical and spiritual reasons to embrace the SEAM values. Responding to employees respectfully, with love, creates a workplace in which people are free to grow intellectually, emotionally, and spiritually. This is the human development — the ultimate goal of SEAM, the development of each person who will then make the workplace more energized, creative, cohesive, successful, and effective.

From time to time, in organizations that undergo a SEAM intervention, we hear the comment that it is easy to tell when people have been exposed to and touched by SEAM, and when they have not. SEAM changes the way managers and employees think. When there is a problem, people touched by SEAM do not look for whom to blame, but rather look for a collaborative way to resolve the problem and succeed together. That may sound like a simple change, yet it is a huge shift in a way people think about work and management. These are the kind of employees who are prepared to work in the future organizations. These are the kind of managers who can create and nurture creative, participative, and highly cohesive teams. These managers are able to make organizations competitive and steer them into the future.

Bibliography

Argyris, C. (1990). *Integrating the Individual and the Organization*. Milton Park, UK: Taylor & Francis.

Argyris, C. (1990). *Overcoming Organizational Defenses*. Upper Saddle River, NJ: Prentice Fall.

Boje, D. & Rosile, G. A. (2003). Comparison of socio-economic and other transorganizational development methods. *Journal of Organizational Change Management, 16*(1), 10–20.

Boje, D. & Rosile, G. A. (2003). Theatrics of SEAM. *Journal of Organizational Change Management, 16*(1), 21–32.

Buono, A. F. & Savall, H. (eds). (2007). ISEOR's socio-economic method. A case of scientific consultancy. In: *Socio-Economic Intervention in Organizations. The Intervener-Researcher and the SEAM Approach to Organizational Analysis*. Charlotte, NC: Information Age Publishing.

Buono, A. F. & Savall, H. (eds). (2015). *The Socio-Economic Approach to Management Revisited: The Evolving Nature of SEAM in the 21st Century*. Charlotte, NC: Information Age Publishing.

Caghasi, J. (2014). SEAM implementation in mergers and acquisitions. In: *Facilitating the Socio-Economic Approach to Management*. Charlotte, NC: Information Age Publishing.

Conbere, J. P. & Heorhiadi, A. (2011). Socio-economic approach to management: A successful systemic approach to organizational change. *Organization Development Practitioner, 43*(1), 6–10.

Conbere, J. P. & Heorhiadi, A. (2016). Magical thinking as organizational dysfunction. *The Theory and Practice of Socio-Economic Management, 1*(2),

28–37. http://resources.css.edu/sbt/seam/articles/volume1/conbere_and_heorhiadi.pdf.

Conbere, J. P. & Heorhiadi, A. (2017). How transformative learning informs the SEAM process. *The Theory and Practice of Socio-Economic Management, 1*(2), 26–35. http://resources.css.edu/sbt/seam/articles/volume1/issue2/conbereheorhiadi.pdf.

Conbere, J. P. & Heorhiadi, A. (2015). Why the socio-economic approach to management remains a well kept secret. *Organization Development Practitioner*, *46*(3), 31–37.

Conbere, J. P., Savall, H. & Heorhiadi, A. (2015). *Decoding the Socio-Economic Approach to Management*. Charlotte, NC: Information Age Publishing.

Daloz, L. A. P. (2000). Transformative learning for the common good. In: *Learning as Transformation*, J. Mezirow (ed.). (pp. 103–125). San Francisco: Jossey-Bass.

Friesenborg, L. (2017). Exposing single-loop learning and the TFW virus: A case study of the Columbia Accident Investigation. *The Theory and Practice of Socio-Economic Management, 1*(2), 36–61. http://sources.css.edu/sbt/seam/articles/volume1/issue2/friesenborg.pdf.

Gall, M. D., Gall, J. P. & Borg, W. R. (2007). *Educational Research: An Introduction* (8th edition). Boston, MA: Allyn-Bacon.

Heorhiadi, A., Conbere, J. P. & Hazelbaker, C. (2014). Virtue vs. virus: Can OD overcome the heritage of scientific management? *Organization Development Practitioner, 46*(3), 27–31.

Heorhiadi, A. & Hartl, R. (2017). Using metaphors and similes to explain the socio economic approach to management. *The Theory and Practice of Socio-Economic Management, 2*(1), 54–64. http://resources.css.edu/sbt/seam/articles/volume1/issue3/heorhiadihartl.pdf.

Heorhiadi, A., La Venture, K. & Conbere, J. P. (2014). What do organizations need to learn to become a learning organization? *Organization Development Practitioner, 46*(2), 5–9.

Herzberg, F. (September–October 1987). One more time: How do you motivate employees? *Harvard Business Review*, *65*(5), 109–120.

Kalnbach, L. & Swenson, D. X. (2017). SEAM in higher education: A case study. *The Theory and Practice of Socio-Economic Management, 1*(2), 16–25. http://resources.css.edu/sbt/seam/articles/volume1/issue2/kalnbachswenson.pdf.

Kennedy, A. (2016). Developing human potential and a learning culture in manufacturing. *The Theory and Practice of Socio-Economic Management, 1*(2), 38–45. http://resources.css.edu/sbt/seam/articles/volume1/kennedy.pdf.

Lewin, K. (1997). *Resolving Social Conflicts and Field Theory in Social Science.* Washington, DC: American Psychological Society.

Likert, R. (1967). *The Human Organization: Its Management and Value.* New York: McGraw-Hill.

MacGregor, D. (1985). *The Human Side of Enterprise*, 25th Anniversary edition. Boston: McGraw-Hill.

Péron, M. & Péron, M. (2003). Post-modernism and socio-economic approach to organizations. *Journal of Organizational Change Management, 16*(1), 49–55.

Quint, S. (2017). The four leaf clover revisited. *The Theory and Practice of Socio-Economic Management, 2*(1), 30–41. http://resources.css.edu/sbt/seam/articles/volume1/issue3/quint.pdf.

Randall, B. (2017). How SEAM addresses the key drivers for employee engagement. *The Theory and Practice of Socio-Economic Management, 2*(1), 42–53. http://resources.css.edu/sbt/seam/articles/volume1/issue3/randall.pdf.

Savall, H. (2017). Macroeconomic roots and fundamentals of the socio-economic approach to management. *The Theory and Practice of Socio-Economic Management, 1*(1), 3–29. http://www.css.edu/about/seam-journal/journal-articles/macroeconomic-roots-and-fundamentals-of-the-socio-economic-approach-to-management.html.

Savall, H. (2003). An update presentation of the socio-economic management model. *Journal of Organizational Change Management, 16*(1), 38–48.

Savall, H. (2010). *Work and People: An Economic Evaluation of Job-Enrichment.* Charlotte, NC: Information Age Publishing. (First published in 1974.)

Savall, H., Conbere, J. P., Heorhiadi, A., Cristallini, V. & Buono, A. F. (eds.) (2014). *Facilitating the Socio-Economic Approach to Management: Results of the First SEAM Conference in North America.* Charlotte, NC: Information Age Publishing.

Savall, H., Péron, M., Zardet, V. & Bonnet, M. (2018). *Socially Responsible Capitalism and Management.* New York: Routledge.

Savall, H. & Zardet, V. (2017). *Strategic Engineering of the Reed — Reflections on Socio-Economic Strategy and Implementation.* Charlotte, NC: Information Age Publishing.

Savall, H. & Zardet, V. (2008). *Mastering Hidden Costs and Socio-Economic Performance.* Charlotte, NC: Information Age Publishing. (First published in French in 1987.)

Savall, H. & Zardet, V. (2011). *Qualimetrics: Observing the Complex Object.* IAP: Charlotte, NC. (First published in French in 2004.)

Savall, H. & Zardet, V. (2013). *Dynamics and Challenges of Tetranormalization.* IAP: Charlotte, NC. (First published in French in 2005.)

Savall, H. & Zardet, V. (2016). The difference between management consultancy and research-intervention. *The Theory and Practice of Socio-Economic Management, 1*(3), 3–15. http://resources.css.edu/sbt/seam/articles/volume1/issue2/savallzardet.pdf.

Savall, H. & Zardet, V. (2016). Strategic Bedrock theory and the cohesion leverage effect. *The Theory and Practice of Socio-Economic Management, 1*(1), 3–15. http://www.css.edu/about/seam-journal/journal-articles/strategic-bedrock-theory.html.

Savall, H., Zardet, V. & Bonnet, M. (2008). *Releasing the Untapped Potential of Enterprises through Socio-Economic Management*. Geneva: International Labor Office, and Ecully, France: ISEOR. (First published in 1974.)

Schein, E. (1992). *Process Consultation Revisited*. Boston: Addison Wesley.

Schein, E. (2009). *The Corporate Culture Survival Guide*. Hoboken, NJ: Wiley.

Schein, E. (2010). *Organizational Culture and Leadership*, Edition 4. Hoboken, NJ: Wiley.

Swanson, R. A. & Holton, E. F. (1999). *Results: How to Assess Performance, Learning, and Perceptions in Organizations*. San Francisco: Berrett-Koehler Publishers.

Weber, M. (2003). *The Protestant Ethic and the Spirit of Capitalism*. Mineola, NY: Dover Publications.

Worley, C., Zardet, V., Bonnet, M. & Savall, A. (2015). *Becoming Agile — How the SEAM Approach to Management Builds Adaptability*. San Francisco: Jossey & Bass.

Yin, R. (2007). *Case Study Research: Design and Methods*, Edition 4. Thousand Oaks, CA: Sage.

Zardet, V. & Voyant, O. (2003). Organizational transformation through the socio-economic approach in an industrial context. *Journal of Organizational Change Management, 16*(1), 56–71.

Dissertations

Baune, C. (2016). *A Phenomonological Research Study about the Experience of Leaders Who Have Led a SEAM Intervention*. [Unpublished doctoral dissertation]. University of St. Thomas, Minneapolis, MN.

Hazelbaker, C. (2014). *Looking for Evidence of the TFW Virus*. [Unpublished doctoral dissertation]. University of St. Thomas, Minneapolis, MN.

Quint, S. (2014). *Development of a Business Case for Investment in Analytic Software: An Organization Development Perspective*. [Unpublished doctoral dissertation]. University of St. Thomas. Minneapolis, MN.

Index

Printed in the United States
By Bookmasters